Travel, the Celebrity Way

by

Dorothea Desforges

Published by Buttercup Press
South Cave, East Yorkshire HU15 2JG

First Published in Great Britain in 2000

Cover by Dorothea Desforges

ISBN 0-9539190-2-1

Gem Desk Top Publishing
Welton, East Yorkshire, HU15 1NP

CONTENTS

ACKNOWLEDGMENTS

I'm indebted to all the personalities who took time to tell me some wonderful anecdotes.

Without their help, I could not have completed this book and now, many charities will benefit from their kindness.

A special thank you to Alan and Shirley Plater, who have supported me throughout my various careers. Love you madly.

And a great big hug to my husband Ray, who when the midnight oil is burning, encourages me with coffee and a wicked grin - Must remember to buy him some pyjamas!

INTRODUCTION

For over twenty years I was a travel agent in Hull. This is probably one of the most enviable jobs going. But it did have its down side - It did!

I've been groped by a gorilla, held captive in Cairo, vandalised in the Virgin Islands (but ***Richard Branson*** came to my rescue) sabataged in a snowstorm and I once mistook a circumcision clinic for a jewellers. ('That's the unkindest cut of all,' said my husband)

Destinations are usually a blur unless I've had an earth moving encounter (not neccessarily of the volcanic variety!)

If I mention the Eternal city of Rome, you will probably think of the Seven Hills, the Vatican or tossing a coin in the Trevi Fountain.

Me? My abiding memory is of an agent from Slough sloping off with a twenty-three year old Italian waiter and returning the following day, beaming brightly on the back of a moped. She was fifty-seven!

I also collect mementoes, my resistance is virtually non-existent when I spot a local market. My bargains vary from the sublime to the ridiculous and I'm always a sucker for a hat. I have small, round, silk hats from China, sombreros from Mexico, yashmaks from Morocco, a straw creation with ears protruding from the crown and I was not a pretty sight in Heathrow trying to navigate the loo door with twelve stetsons dancing around my person.

Some travellers go merrily on their way year after year. Not for them an army of ants in their best knickers, or a loo that only flushes at 3am. And do they ever travel during the strike of French traffic control? Do they 'eck as like.

Does this sort of thing happen to the rich and famous, and where do they go for relaxation?

Have they ever endured a camp site in the middle of the night, trying to find the dug out latrines in the pouring rain, while being attacked by a swarm of killer mosquitoes in the nether regions? And I'll bet their villa for eight really DOES sleep eight, not five like mine, unless you count the two sunbeds on the patio and the exotic circular bath, which, with a blanket on the bottom, doubled beautifully as a bed, as long as your toes didn't attach themselves to the taps during the night.

I always thought wet and warm meant my tea!

During twenty years of gallivanting I've met some famous, infamous and celebrated personalities. I was regaled with tales of hysterical honeymoons, cocky camels and paralytic porters, also a fair share of murderous mountains, broken bones and galloping goats.

And as I've mentioned I've had my share of tortuous travel, so I'll toss in a few shenanigans of my own.

Alan Plater, the playwright has visited many varied and exotic locations, often to research for a film or television project.

He confessed that much of his life had been 'one long holiday'.

"This year I'm celebrating forty years as a professional writer or - to express it another way - forty years without a proper job. That was my aim from the beginning. Along the way there have been many disappointments and a few betrayals but compared with, say, mining or deep-sea fishing, the job is a doddle: one long holiday.

It has taken me to an amazing variety of places, and from this distance I have to concentrate very hard to remember whether what took me there was work or play. The two things are interchangeable and, as Noel Coward once said: fun isn't only fun - only work is fun.

Essentially I am a wimp. I was once asked to do a research trip up the Amazon. The conversation went something like this:

"How far up the Amazon?"

"A long way."

"As in sleeping in a hammock in the jungle with nothing between me and nature?"

"That's about it."

"And no room service?"

"Definitely no room service."

"Try ***Harold Pinter.***"

In the event, another writer (male, but not Harold Pinter) took on the assignment and was helicoptered out within twenty-four hours in a state of terminal hysteria. Yet another writer (female) took the job on and enjoyed every minute of it.

Heritage leaves me cold but I love places where you can breathe in the history: whether it's Tennessee Williams' streetcar in New Orleans, the cathedral of St. Magnus in Orkney - or the erudite Israeli guide in Jerusalem who spoke lovingly of Moses and David as if they'd just slipped around the corner.

All that being so, when it comes to drawing up the top ten list of holiday places known and loved, it comes out this way, no special order: Florence, Paris, Venice, New Orleans, Orkney, Raratonga, Sydney, Northumberland, Jamaica...and Jarrow."

Ronan Keating, considered the nicest man in pop admits he loves travelling. When he was asked what he considered the perks of fame, he answered: "The travelling is fantastic. I have visited some beautiful and interesting countries such as Bali, Bangkok and America. I've also been to Paris many times. I love it and I have many friends there. If I wasn't doing this for a living, there's no way I'd have got to see so much of the world, so I'm grateful for that. Luckily I never get lonely when I'm travelling because Yvonne and our baby son Jack travel with me most of the time."

Harry Secombe says he loves to see a landscape of wooded hills. The late ***Frankie Howerd***, didn't mind where he was as long as he could see beautiful sunrises and sunsets. ***Lauren Bacall*** likes to watch the sea and a sky full of stars. And need I tell you what ***Patrick Moore*** enjoys. "A total eclipse of the sun."

As they say there's no accounting for taste.

The wonderful comedian ***Bob Monkhouse*** asked me if I knew the definition of a European. I admitted I didn't.

It's someone who has:
The ability to work as hard as the British,
The organisation of the Italians,
The sobriety of the Irish,
The modesty of the French,
The broad horizons of the Luxembourgoise,
The prudishness of the Danes,
The cheerful outlook of the Norwegians,
The humour of the Germans,
The generosity of the Dutch,
He is in short, a Belgian.

Maureen Lipman, a Hull girl like me, apart from being a celebrated actress is also a comedienne, columnist, author and a wonderful raconteur.

"Mountains and scenery are not for me," said Maureen. "I get much more pleasure from watching and listening to fellow guests and holidaymakers. Eavesdropping is one of my favourite pastimes.

"I go round for hours with an inane grin on my face, when I hear snippets which are pure joy. I remember in a restaurant once I heard a ladies voice call out,'Excuse me, but can I have some coffee without cream?"I'm very sorry,' said the waiter, we don't have cream, you'll have to have it without milk."

A girl after my own heart. Life is often so bizarre, it wouldn't be included in your wildest dreams.

I once saw ***Spike Milligan*** being interviewed on television and he was asked about holidays and true to form cracked a gag. "Have you heard about the Irish pilot who had to eject from his plane, as he was plummeting earthwards, he saw another Irishman speeding upwards, "Do you know anything about parachutes?' the pilot shouted. "No" he answered, "Do you know anything about gas stoves?"

Hold on tight it's time to travel, the celebrity way.

AUSTRALIA

I'd been invited to dinner by my friend ***Will Fyffe*** Jnr and his partner ***Anthea Askey*** and some of the cast and musicians from the pantomime which was being staged at the Hull New Theatre. I was delighted to find I had been placed next to ***Rolf Harris***, but I'm afraid we turned out to be terrible dinner companions. We chatted incessantly the whole evening. I'm a great admirer of his painting and when I mentioned it, he asked the waitress for some paper and proceeded to give me an art lesson. I failed miserably. He rewarded me with a pen and ink drawing/cartoon, of myself and my husband.

Rolf told me about the problems he has when touring, mainly with luggage. He recalled the time he was invited to do a month long tour of Australia.

"I arrived at Heathrow Airport and checked in with one large suitcase and two fold-over suit cases. They tied the two fold-over holdalls together, attaching a single label to cover them both. I asked if it was all right going in the hold and only one label. The clerk said I wasn't to worry, they'd look after it. I still thought it a bit odd but didn't like to say anything as I was sure they knew what they were doing.

When I arrived in Perth, no fold-over luggage. The airline took the number of my hotel and said they would call as soon they had located the missing baggage. I told them it was an absolute emergency as my tour was due to start in four days and not only was my tailor-made evening suit in the bags, but the mainstay of my act, the 'Jake The Peg' suit was missing. I couldn't believe it, as I'm sure you know it's an integral part of my show. People come expecting it, like me playing the digeridoo.

I rang twice a day every day, but it never did turn up."

"It must have been a nightmare," I said.

"You're right, it was. I eventually had to have another one made up. It arrived at the very last minute and as you can imagine it was slightly different and I found it difficult to swing that extra leg. It was like an amputation. Most peculiar."

So if any of you come across a fellah in a beige mac. and an extra leg, give Rolf a ring.

My son Adam had decided he would take time out to back-pack around Australia before taking up his place at drama school. He took various jobs to pay his way. He found that having an English accent was a definite turn-off to would be employers, so acquired the local vernacular pretty swiftly.

One job he obtained was washing glasses in a bar. He got talking to a local and asked if there was any cheap accommodation available. "Don't ask me," said the local, "I haven't been home for three days."

Adam thought he must live in the bush, so asked how far his homestead was. A weary hand waved in the general direction of East.

"How many kilometres?" asked Adam.

"None you silly bugger, that's my house across the street."

Another job proved quite lucrative. He was employed as a courier for a television company based in Perth. After chatting up the receptionist, he ended up being offered work in several commercials. One was for an advertisement which entailed lying in a bed being comforted by a bronzed female body. Talk about money for old rope.

"Oh, no it wasn't" he wailed, "they found a redback in the loo and if you get a nip from one of them you're a dead man."

I would get sporadic phone-calls - usually asking for money - and just to let me know where he was.

One call from Perth, told me about a sign he's seen hung up in a small shop.

'If you steal from this shop, we'll break your legs.'

"Why anybody would even try to pinch anything I can't imagine," said Adam.

"Why, what were they selling?" I asked.

He chuckled. "Would you believe lavatory bowls!"

On Christmas day he rang and said he was at a barbi. enjoying 'snaggers and chuck' - sausages and chicken to the un-initiated - with some other back-packers on a mile long beach and admitted it wasn't the same. "But it does have its good points Mum, there's hundreds of females here, all topless. It's a bit like picking your way across a field of poached eggs, some done, some still raw."

For a Christmas present, I'd sent over some money and he used it for taking scuba diving lessons. He said it was worth every penny, "Especially getting the opportunity to swim with giant turtles. A mind blowing experience."

All in all, a trip he'd recommend to anyone.

He'd been instructed to ring me when he arrived back in London so I could meet him off the train. I knew his six-months visa was due to expire any day, so was waiting for that phone call.

Picture the scene: Saturday lunchtime, Ray and I were running late, very late, for a wedding in 45 minutes time. There was a loud knocking at the front. I muttered under my breath and tutted my way to the door. I opened it to find a tall, rangy individual sporting a full beard and moustache, wearing a long bushman's coat and stetson. I was just about to say, "sorry we don't want any," when I recognised my one and only itinerant son.

The poor thing was dragged inside, a fiver thrust into his hand and he was told to "get some fish and chips" and loving parents disappeared in a puff of smoke up the drive.

When we returned four hours later, he was in an armchair, still unshaven and an empty plate with a few fish remains lingering on the floor and two very contented Siamese cats prostrate on his comatose body.

He still dines out on the saga of his returning home after a gruelling thirty-six hour journey and having been away for over six months, was dismissed as a vagrant by his ever loving mother.

Peter Byrne, who became a household name in 'Dixon Of Dock Green,' and 'Bread,' admits one of his favourite hobbies is scuba diving, so he was delighted when he was invited by ***Derek Nimmo*** to tour Australia and the Far East.

"To dive off the Great Barrier Reef had been a dream of mine for years, so I was thrilled to bits when I saw Queensland was on the itinerary.

"We started the tour in the Far East and the hotels we stayed in were so luxurious, they had to be at least nine star!

"We eventually made Australia (I nearly asked him, out of what, but thought better of it) and I got my chance to sample my dream."

Before I continue with Peter's story, I thought you might like a few fascinating facts about the Great barrier Reef.

It's actually a chain of islands about 1,250 miles long and is believed to be the world's largest living organism - I had to spell that carefully! - and forms a natural breakwater, and the coral rock forms a structure larger than all the human made structures on earth, combined.

Beware the full moon in November, because, annually, 135 species of hard coral release their eggs and sperm for fertilisation and the sea turns pink. The phenomenon, is one of the wonders of the natural world but was not discovered until 1983. It is triggered by a mechanism dependant solely on the Moon, tides and the water temperatures.

But the reef is in dire danger. It's been reported that large numbers of starfish, have infested over 30% of the reef. In fact I was reading recently that scientists are certain the entire reef will disappear by 2050.

Just thought you might be interested, anyway back to Peter.

I asked him if he enjoyed the experience.

"It was absolutely breathtaking." he said, "but I learnt an invaluable lesson out there."

"Oh, what was that?"

"Coral. It might look beautiful and fragile but it can be lethal."

"Really, how?"

"I'd been diving and having a wonderful time but when I eventually surfaced, I was told I had numerous ugly looking cuts along my back, but I hadn't felt a thing. The Australians told me to stay in the water for another twenty minutes, so that it could cauterise the wounds."

"Ooh, that sounds nasty."

"To be honest I didn't realise how bad they were. Some of the gashes were so deep, they wouldn't stop bleeding, so as soon as we got back to the hotel they called a doctor."

"Did that put you off?" I asked.

"Not a bit of it, in fact it was worth every scratch."

About a week later, he had another scary incident. But this time nothing to do with coral.

One of the young girls in the play had mentioned she had always wanted to swim with dolphins and Peter had seen some publicity about a nearby sea-world, so he offered to take her.

He told me: "We went along the next day. I introduced myself to the dolphin trainer and explained the girls ambition.

He was delighted to help. After changing, she lowered herself into the pool.

She seemed a bit apprehensive. I watched as the animal nudged her on her arm. 'He wants you to swim with him,' shouted the keeper, so she moved around the pool, all the time the dolphin was gliding effortlessly beside her, uttering those familiar clicking noises."

He smiled at the memory.

"You should have seen the pair of them frolicking in the water, even though it seemed sort of muddy coloured and made it rather eerie. Most odd. But the girl seemed oblivious to her surroundings. She seemed to be in another world. It was as if she was entranced. Then I noticed the time and yelled for her to come out."

"No way," she shouted This is absolute heaven. You have to come in and try it.

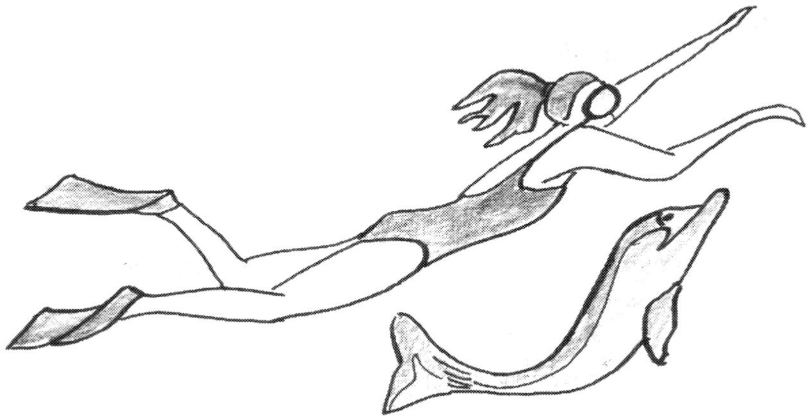

She'd already been in the pool over an hour and the evenings performance was looming closer and closer. She kept insisting I join her, so I relented and quickly putting on my trunks, slid into the water."

Peter gave a small shudder and shaking his head, said: "You wouldn't believe the change that came over that dolphin. It left the girl's side and started swimming very, very slowly towards me. It stopped about thirty feet away and I know it sounds silly but it was so ominous, I felt very uncomfortable, it was uttering such unpleasant noises. I decided to climb out. Suddenly the dolphin, making horrific screeching noises headed towards me. There was hardly a ripple as this torpedo sped through the muddy water, looking for a direct hit on my midriff. I was frozen in absolute terror.

"Do you know?" he asked, "their noses are like iron. They could smash a human to shreds without any trouble at all. But," he told me, "the only thing that flashed through my mind at that moment was. "Oh, please God, don't let me die in brown Windsor soup."

He truly thought he was experiencing his last moments and the beast had every intention of killing him, but at the very last moment, this great silver mammal, swerved past his rigid body.

"I couldn't believe I was still intact. I scrambled back onto the concrete surround. My heart was pounding and I was trembling. Looking back to the pool area, I saw the girl was again playing happily with the dolphin."

She had been completely unaware of the danger Peter had been in. When he told her, she said, "It was nothing to worry about. It was just a little warning."

"Some warning." said Peter. "Tell him it worked."

I told him that I had recently visited Brazil and while I was relaxing on a beach near San Paulo, I got chatting to the guide and he told me that dolphins who swim happily with females, will consider any males who enter their territory as rivals. They had a wild dolphin called Tiao, who swam in their bay and so they imposed a ban in the area, but no-one would believe this beautiful creature could cause harm, even though they were told he weighed over 35 stone.

He told me: "Twenty-seven men who ignored the warnings, were attacked. Many seriously and one actually died from his injuries."

I also couldn't resist telling Peter about an article I'd read. A biologist had discovered that dolphins are now being seen in a new light, as killers! They possess a darker side not before recognised.

It suggested that people who love dolphins uncritically are a bunch of sentimental idiots. It went on, 'If you get on a head-on position the dolphin may interpret it as aggressive or threatening so always put yourself at an oblique angle to the animal.

"Now you tell me," said a shocked Peter.

Jilly Johnson, the actress and model was born in Australia with the Great Barrier Reef on her doorstep and admits: "My early life was one long holiday. But when I was nine, we moved to England. But I can understand why people fall in love with my country and especially that wonderful reef."

Clive James was interviewing ***Peter Ustinov*** on television and Mr Ustinov was recounting the tale about the time he was invited on a kangeroo shoot.

"The thought appalled me, but I didn't want to appear rude to my host so I went along. Thank God they never found any, mind you we did find a rabbit which had been run over by a jeep, so I returned the triumphant hunter."

By the way do you know how the kangaroo got its name?

Well the story goes that Captain Cook had landed and was carefully sketching all that he saw. Nearby an old wrinkled Aboriginal man was intently observing Captain Cook, so the captain went over to him and nodded in the direction of the Kangaroo and waving his arms in what he thought were descriptive gestures, asked what it was. The old man slowly put down his knife, looked long and hard at the nearby animal, then back to Cook, he thought for a few minutes, then muttered, "Kangaroo."

Captain Cook hastily entered this in his diary, thanked the Aborigine and headed back to his ship.

It's only recently while researching into the Aboriginal language, that they found out what it really meant, "No bloody idea," or words to that effect!

It must have been one helluva job for the researcher, because in 1770, when Captain Cook arrived in Botany Bay, it was estimated there were over 35,000 Aboriginal people and between them they spoke 250 languages.

A story about a client of mine I thought you might like.

Rose was eighty years old, but had decided to emigrate to her daughter's, who lived in a small town called Bullcreek, just outside Perth. She had her own small place in the grounds, but she couldn't settle. She stayed for three years but then decided to return to England.

When she returned she came in the shop to tell me all about it. "The creepy-crawlies were like something out of a horror movie," she said, "and I spent half my time sitting in a cold bath to cool down and I know you'll think I'm a dotty old woman, but most of all I hated their watery, tasteless bacon. I used to dream of thick Danish rashers sizzling in the pan and that decided me. I wanted to end my final few years with bacon butties, green fields and rain."

I was visiting the Gold Coast and received an invitation from the tourist board which read, 'Around The World in a Meal.'

Before dinner we were given a talk, followed by an hour of promotional videos. The guy introducing the evening told us:

"Our product is virtually unique." Now was it or wasn't it?

Later a Qantas airline official went into great detail about:

"Passengers who don't just stop wherever they arrive." I think I know what he meant.

By the way, why is there no 'u' in the national airline Qantas? Because it stands for, Queensland and Northern Territory Aerial Services.

Now if the conversation starts to lag...

Anyway back to that meal.

The preliminaries over and two hundred travel agents were ushered into the dining room. There was a huge buffet and among the delights were;

Bombay Duck.
Yorkshire Pudding.
Lancashire Hot-Pot.

Russian Roulade

Swiss Roll.

Nice Biscuits - I felt that was scraping the barrel - oh well please yourselves.

Frogs legs.

Rice.

Hamburgers.

Hungarian Goulash.

Canadian Pumpkin pie.

Well they tried bless'em. Though I was slightly confused with a display of 'selected, assorted lettuces.'

While I was on the Gold Coast I met ***Paul Daniels***. He is not only a spectacular magician but he is always ready with a quip and has the gift of the gab second to none. He can out dazzle and outwit any heckler who tries to take him on.

I have met him on a couple of occasions, but the first was on Australia's Gold Coast as an ambassador for the American Express credit card. He happily posed for photographs and collared anyone who walked within five yards. I only had a short time to chat and he asked me if I'd heard about the young priest who was flying for the first time to a convention in Rome.

"It was a very bumpy flight and lightening could be seen flashing in the midnight sky. Everyone was asked to 'belt up,' in the nicest possible way of course" said Paul.

"Ashen faced passengers were sitting stiffly to attention in their seats and staring straight ahead, suddenly a voice loudly proclaimed: "Well I've read the book, I've seen the movie, now it looks like I'm going to meet the author."

And with a big grin and a cheery wave he was on his way.

SYDNEY

In 1999, they were holding local elections and the voters had to struggle with a ballot paper the size of a bath towel. The document was a metre long and contained the names of more than 600 candidates. About 80 fringe groups included the "Make Billionaires Pay more Tax" party, also the "Sack Them All" party.

One of he scrutineers said: "It was a nightmare. We had to go out and get extra chairs to help the frail and elderly record their votes."

The playwright ***Alan Plater***, was invited to Australia for a three month teaching stint and he loved every minute. He told me: "Of all the places we've visited in the world, Sydney is the one we yearn to go back to. The landscape is handsome, it almost doesn't matter what the developers do to the city, nature wins in the end. The people are generous, funny and rude, and they touch their forelocks to nobody."

I was listening to the broadcaster ***Lynne Parsons*** on radio 2 and she was telling her listeners the sort of questions that had been received by the Sydney Tourist Board, prior to the 2000 Olympics.

"Can you see kangaroos running around in the street?" asked one hopeful. Another mentioned that he always watched neighbours, but he'd never seen it rain on television, so wanted to know: "How do your plants grow?"

And a similar cock-eyed question from Len of Salisbury. "I like sailing," he told them, "but I've never seen it windy on TV, so does everyone have to have powered boats?"

He's obviously never heard of 'Doctor Freemantle,' a brute which blusters across the Western tip of Australia - I was there at the start of the Round The World yacht race and it was ferocious.

AUSTRIA

MAYERHOFEN

A very picturesque resort with something for everyone all year round, and I can recommend their apres-ski!

The first time I visited the resort was with my husband and two year old son. We'd been having a leisurely stroll along the river path when Adam was stung by a bee and his thumb came up like a small balloon. I trotted off to the local apothecary to see if I could obtain some soothing balm.

Have you noticed, that as a general rule it is the women who are left to discover the native tongue. Men seem to believe females were born linguists and should take to it like the maternal instinct.

Here I was in the shop, without a word of German, except, nein, gut morgan, mein herr and achtung, which I feared would not stand me in good stead with the local populace.

The chemist spoke even less English. Now was the time to put all that drama training into practise. I aeroplaned around the shop, arms akimbo, buzzing loudly. Suddenly I grabbed the man's hand and bit his thumb.

When he yelled, I nodded enthusiastically.

He got the message and produced a tube of cream. He would accept no payment. Well I don't suppose you often get cabaret and your thumb bitten for a tube of salve do you?

That cream lasted for two years. Even neighbours came to borrow it. I think I can safely say, every single child in our street had some rubbed on their backsides at some time or other.

I'd better explain. Our garden had been invaded by ants. Armies of them.

The second time I visited the resort, it was the depths of winter and I was a guest of Thomson Holidays.

One night we were taken for a toboggan ride. It was gone 9pm when we were taken to the top of a steep - make that vertical - hill, come mountain. While we were waiting for the sleds to be arranged, another mini-bus arrived and a group of German travel agents piled out. The mother of all snowball fights ensued. When we were all exhausted and covered in snow we were told to get a partner for the sled ride. The Thomson rep. ***Tony Iredale***, (who now owns a travel agency in Huddersfield and is the travel expert on Yorkshire Television) shouted "Come on Dot, we'll show'em." I climbed behind him on this small 'craft'. Guides at the top gave us each a hot gluewein and as we handed back the glass, we were unceremoniously kicked off down the slope. The whole thing was floodlit, with numerous bends. Sleds in front of us were going quite sedately the 'riders' digging their ski boots in order to halt their decent. No such fineries with Tony. We stuck our feet out in front of us and as we caught up with the slower sleds, Tony would scream, 'Move it, move it," they would tumble into the side while we shot past them like a bullet. As we were careering around a bend, we saw a huge arrow pointing right. Underneath was written: 'Kamikaze run'. Ski boots thudded into the icy run, as Tony lit out to the right. We hit a road further down at the speed of sound and ploughed into the bank of snow at the side. Three more sleds from our party hurtled down after us and also thudded into the drift, catapulting us all into a chaotic jumble. As we were all scrambling to our feet, Kathy, one of the Thomson staff came down on her own but she was thrown out so violently that she ended up on top of the snow bank, with a precipitous, thousand feet drop beckoning below. We all collapsed in uncontrollable laughter. We eventually made it all in one piece to the bottom windswept and dishevelled but gloriously happy. A welcome hostelry was waiting with more hot Gluewein. I got such a penchant for the stuff, I was nick-named the Gluewein Queen.

SALZBURG

This really is a spectacular city, compact and tangibly prosperous, presided over by the Hohensalzburg, an austere white-walled fortress rising from sheer cliffs. It has rightly earned the nickname "Northern Rome," as it is rife with baroque churches. They are as richly decorated as the cakes so beloved of the Austrians.

Famous for being the birthplace of Mozart, concerts are held year round, even buskers attempt an aria from The Magic Flute.

I was on a coach tour and had visited the souvenir shop next to his birthplace and then we'd wandered off, but when we returned to the coach, one of our party who we'd left lingering over Mozart T-shirts, told us the shop had entertained a famous visitor when we'd gone. None other than ***Arnold Schwarzenegger***, who was sifting through opera C.D's. He was accompanied by his wife and daughter who was tugging his sleeve and yelling. "Daddee! I want an ice-cream NOW!

Book a Sound Of Music tour. I walked next to a Greek woman who insisted on singing. "a flibbertigibbet, a will-o-the-wisp, a clown,' throughout the tour. It was made infinitely more interesting by our guide, a very camp, Burt Reynolds look alike. We visited the Abbey, the villa and the church, even the gazebo where Liesl and her boyfriend Rolf, sang "I am 16 going on 17."

We were not allowed inside as evidently an 80 year old tourist had leapt from one bench to another in youthful exuberance only to fall and break her hip.

VIENNA

When ***Graham Greene*** went to the city in 1948 seeking out a story for a screenplay, the hostilities of the Second World War had left the buildings in ruins or damaged. But thanks to a remarkable rebuilding effort, war damage is no longer apparent. Following the success of the film you can now go on a Third Man themed tour.

I recommend you have nerves of steel and, ideally, a weak sense of smell when you visit the underground chambers which saw the demise of Harry Lime.

Just a warning be prepared for a gunshot and lots of smoke and when they tell you to 'run,' run!

Dame Thora Hird recalled a trip to Vienna. "I was browsing around in a tourist shop when the German shopkeeper got irate because I was admiring a lovely scarf and didn't have enough money to buy it. When I walked out, the assistant came after me asking why I hadn't bought the scarf and saying the purchase had gone through the computer. 'What am I going to tell the manager?' she said. I just looked at her and said: "Tell him who won the war."

Just thought you'd like to know that if you are ever caught short in Vienna and need to spend a schilling, the city authorities have used the World Wide Web to publicise a map - with all 340 of the city's toilets marked - So if you have one of those familiar stomach churning moments, all you need to do is visit the web.

BAHAMAS

I listened with horror to the story agony aunt, ***Claire Raynor*** had to tell, as I've visited the island and had a wonderful time, finding the locals, friendly and obliging, but Claire found a very different story.

"When we went to the island, we were really looking forward to a luxurious time, but when we got there it was unbelievably awful. The hotel was a nightmare. The plughole in our washbasin wasn't connected to the pipework, and the water flooded into the bedroom. I went for a swim in the pool and came face to face with a rat - I did the fastest backflip you've ever seen! When we tried to take a day trip away from the hotel the taxi driver announced he hated 'honkies' and refused to go faster than 5mph. Worst of all, we'd treated ourselves to a fortnight and couldn't get an early flight home, so we were forced to stay."

John Prescott MP and his beautiful wife Pauline were on a business trip to the island. One day, completely free of meetings, John decided the perfect way to explore the area untouched by tourists was by motorbike.

They found out very swiftly that progress was going to be very slow. The 'roads' were atrocious and littered with potholes.

"Negotiating the abundant lumps, bumps and holes was quite exciting," said John. "In fact we were quite enjoying the thrill of it, when suddenly the back wheel caught in a deep rut and we were catapulted onto the road."

After the initial shock they dusted themselves down and reviewed the damage. John had escaped relatively unscathed with just a few minor bumps and bruises, but Pauline, his wife, had a nasty gash on her leg.

The bleeding was stemmed but walking was difficult. John told me: "The bike had a twisted back wheel so was un-rideable and it had started to rain. I told my wife to stay where she was and I'd go and try to find help."

Mr Prescott trudged off back the way they'd come, while Pauline tried to make herself comfortable under a tree, to protect her from the downpour. She was getting wetter and more anxious by the minute. Her leg was very sore and she was starting to feel the bumps and bruises. Wet and miserable she suddenly heard the sound of an engine. "I was going to rush out onto the road," said Mrs Prescott, "But then I realised it was coming from the opposite direction. I'm afraid I panicked and dragged the bike behind the tree and sat cowering in the thick, wet undergrowth."

"What happened?"

"Nothing. It was just a rusty little car. I watched it bump its way past my hiding place and disappear up the road and I'm afraid I began to cry," she confessed.

"How long did you have to wait?"

"Oh not very long. It was only a few minutes after that I heard another engine. This time from the right direction. I daren't come out in case it wasn't John. But it was. I was so glad to see him, I ran out and flung my arms around him."

John took up the story. "I'd managed to persuade this guy to go back up the road to pick up Pauline and the bike. Except all he had was a small, very old, very dilapidated pick-up truck with only room for one in front." He laughed. "The expression on the doorman's face was priceless, when this ramshackle heap of rust pulled up at the hotel's swish entrance. He didn't recognise us at first and I think he was very near to telling us to get lost, when he realised who we were."

Mr Prescott and his wife both agreed that "After a long soak in the bath, it was all soon forgotten."

But I bet it took a while for the doorman to forget his encounter with the Deputy Prime Minister of Britain's Labour Party.

"I'd never even contemplated the Bahamas, " said ***Adele Silva***, the Emmerdale actress, But my stepsister, Elaine suggested it and so off I went.

I was always impressed by the blue of the Mediterranean, but the Caribbean was something else. I can only call it magical.

I'm afraid I did nothing but laze around on the beach. I didn't even go clubbing in Nassau, the capital."

Adele was asked if she liked getting a tan. "I always try to get a fabulous tan, but I'm afraid it was so hot, I stayed on a sunbed far too long."

"Does that mean you got burnt?"

"Yes, on my cleavage. But I stupidly popped the blisters and ended up with little white patches all over my chest."

"Anything else that you can tell us about?"

"Just that I really loved the island. Oh, I know, one day I saw a man feeding the sharks. He was attached to a rope and I watched him as he waded out into the water. Suddenly you could see the fins coming towards him. Then they'd pull him back - pretty sharpish. Just watching was really scary."

CAMPING

C*hrista Akroyd*, the Yorkshire Television presenter, told her co-presenter, ***Mike Morris***, that she remembered a time the family went camping in France. "There were molehills everywhere," she said. People were hitting the animals over the head with cricket bats. But otherwise we had a lovely time."

Mike's expression said it all.

Billy Murray, who plays Det. Sgt. Beech in The Bill and also starred in the movie Essex Boys, says camping was one of his earliest recollections of holidays.

"My Auntie Lil and Uncle Sid invited me to join their family holiday to Pevensey Bay in Sussex. I remember being spoiled rotten all week with ice-creams and candyfloss. On our first expedition to the beach, I managed to get covered in tar. I don't know how my aunt managed, but she cleaned me up without a problem."

Two families from Beverley, East Yorkshire, decided they would sample the 'delights' of camping.

They arrived at the campsite and proceeded to put up the tents. All went well and they even had time to prepare a meal.

The dads decided they would go exploring with the children, while the mums - who else? - cleared up.

When all was tidied away, the mums were shattered and decided to go to bed. They said their good-nights and climbed into their respective tents, and after snuggling into the sleeping bag, settled down on the lilo and fell soundly asleep.

When the two families returned, they could find no trace of mum number two. Everyone spread out in different directions, even mum number one was woken from her slumbers to help.

They searched around the tents, engaging other campers in the search. After an hour everyone was getting increasingly concerned, so they all went back to tent number two to discuss what tactics to try next.

Husband number two tried to move the fly flap, to make room for the rest of the party. The heap suddenly moved all on its own. It was his long lost wife.

She'd rolled off the lilo and onto the ground and as she'd snuggled deep into her sleeping bag under the flap, no-one could see her and she'd slept soundly through the whole episode.

I was listening to ***Sara Kennedy*** on her Radio 2, morning show, when she told the following story, sent to her by one of her Dawn Patrol listeners

Keith and his wife had decided to go camping in Norfolk, but forgot the tentpegs, so Keith went into a general store opposite the camp site and asked for six tent pegs. "How large?" asked the forbidding lady at the counter. Keith spread his hands to about a foot apart and said, "About this big." She gave him a funny look and went into the back of the shop. She returned and slapped a small box on the counter. She was still glowering, when she asked for £2.60.

Keith looked at the box. It was a packet of tampons - large size!

Race Davies, an accomplished actress, who originally played Jackie Owen in Eastenders - says she vividly remembers when the family went camping in Spain.

"I would be about four at the time and one night we were woken by my dad Jeffrey, who told us,'Come on! You all have to get up and dig a trench.' There'd been such heavy rain that the tent was in danger of collapsing or being washed away. Dad was more worried than he let on but everyone helped. Even me. I was given a spoon to dig with!"

I know how they felt. It was over thirty years ago when two of our friends persuaded us to join them on a camping holiday.

Ray had grave doubts from the beginning. Room service and delivery of the morning paper are essential ingredients of any holiday to my husband. We headed to the Lake Distinct at Easter. Need I say more. My lilo kept deflating and the tent was being bombarded with torrential rain and I could hear water plopping relentlessly. Suddenly I jerked upright, that relentless plop was inside! But where? I tried to see where it might be accumulating. It had found the perfect spot. Ray's boots! They were full. Now I knew when he found them he would not be a happy bunny. It was 3.30am, but I quietly lit the paraffin stove and after tipping the water out held them over the flames for over two hours, desperately trying to dry them out before he woke.

By 10am the site was a quagmire. Ray helped push all the other cars off the field, when it was our turn, we were stranded. Our friend couldn't help either, he had a bad back. A nearby farmer saw our plight and pulled us out with his tractor.

Oh, by the way, we had our six-month old son with us and he slept blissfully through the lot and no, my husband still hasn't forgiven me for saying yes to Bert and Kay.

CANADA

A bit of geography for you.

Quebec is Canada's biggest province, it is seven times the size of Great Britain and Quebec City, founded in 1608, is Canada's oldest city.

Also did you know that Montreal derives its name from a volcano, long extinct, called Mount Royal?

And Toronto can boast the world's tallest free standing structure, the CN Tower. It takes 58 seconds to ride to the top in its glass fronted lifts. It also boasts the world's highest and largest revolving restaurant where one revolution takes 72 minutes. Canadian refer to the city as the 'people City,' because its inhabited by over 60 different ethnic groups.

Oh by the way it's original nickname was, Hogtown.

There don't you feel better for that?

A gentleman had come into the office to ask if I could tell him what time a flight would arrive in Montreal.

He hadn't booked with us, so I got the airline manual to check, found the relevant page and asked my client. "Who are you flying with sir?"

He looked rather taken aback at my question, but answered firmly, "My sister Mavis."

A few weeks earlier a lady, who had also booked to go to Montreal, was very concerned about flying for the first time. She came in about three days before departure and asked if she could book a seat. "Sorry," I told her, "But you can't do it in advance. They're allocated at the airport."

"But what if they're all gone, when I get there," she wailed. "I don't want to stand all that way."

The Queen visited a confectionery factory while touring Newfoundland and was particularly interested in what one of the workers was doing.

"What exactly do you make here?" asked the Queen.

"About thirteen dollars an hour," replied the girl.

Alan Plater was invited to Northern Ontario to do research on the notorious character 'Grey Owl,' the Englishman who so successfully masqueraded as an Indian for many years. The movie was released in 2000 directed by ***Sir Richard Attenborough*** and starring ***Pierce Brosman.*** It was an instant hit and everything Alan predicted it would be. The playwright said he had a wonderful time. "Canadians," he said, "are of course, the most polite people in the world: they even watch baseball politely. This quality is celebrated beautifully in the TV series Due South."

He met some fascinating characters and he couldn't believe the beauty of the country. He told me: "Canada comes at you thick and fast and I can't think of a better place to take notes for forthcoming scripts. There was a great deal of laughter." He smiled and added. "Usually at my expense and usually about bears, moose or johns. But I learnt a great deal and found the whole episode a fascinating insight into another world and culture."

One old timer he met was the 'Beaver man'. He lived about twenty miles outside Toronto and made wild life documentaries. He had hand-reared some of the animals and he trained them specifically for film making. "They respond to action and cut." Alan giggled. "Everytime he picked one up, it squeaked, but I must admit they are very photogenic creatures."

I asked if he'd met any Indians.

"I did and I learnt quite a lot about Indian culture. I asked one how someone became Chief. Evidently it was by general consensus and it never, ever goes to the one who wants to be chief. I was told: 'If he wants it, he's definitely the wrong man for the job."

Alan went on to tell me he'd found out that; "Irish immigrants had taught the Indians to play the fiddle Irish style and they still have many sensational Indian fiddle players."

Maybe, but if Alan had travelled across to Saskatchewan, he might have found a few ancestors who had been taught by my Uncle Herman.

He'd arrived as a settler in 1904 and quickly made friends with the Indians. His first job was helping build a mission school for a nearby reservation - he was a craftsman carpenter - and after work, he and his brother Allan would sit outside their tent and play, with about two hundred Indians, listening, squatting on the hillock behind. Although I don't quite know what they would have made of songs like, Alice Blue Gown, I'll Take You Home Again Kathleen and The Road To Mandalay.

Uncle Herman said he taught many young bucks English.

Picture the scene.

Uncle Herman walking along a dusty road. Fleet Foot, a young brave approaches.

Herman: "Ey up lad, ist tha reet?"

Fleet Foot: "Ee, by gum lad, I am that."

Who said you can't rewrite history!

Uncle Allan (Herman's brother) told me all the Plains Indians used to describe the white settlers as'Mooniass.'

I've designated a whole chapter in my book The Touchwood Trail, to their escapades with the Indians.

Now lets fast forward ninety years to continue Mr Plater's exploits.

He said he was amused to see a place name but not a house in sight. He found out it was usually just a stop for hunters and fishermen.

He went on to tell me: "I took a flight in a small plane called a Beaver. It was a very interesting two hours, with only an occasional bump. Although I did have one scary moment when the pilot banked steeply towards a lake. I gulped very hard but I was very brave and said nothing. It turned out he was just checking to see if one of his colleagues had arrived safely. I did wonder why he couldn't just lean over and have a look, but I didn't like to ask."

I asked Alan if this was the main way he'd travelled about, as I knew some of the areas were almost inaccessible.

"I travelled on planes, trains and in a few cars," he told me. "I thought we were really in the back of beyond, but one day while I waiting at a small rail station, I saw a clerk carrying a piece of paper with my name on it! I tapped him on the shoulder and said, 'that's me.' The message said I should ring Anne-Marie and gave a phone number."

This was a girl from the TV company, who had commissioned him to do the Grey Owl story and had accompanied him at the start of his journey.

"Anne Marie told me they'd had a call from BBC TV in Newcastle, where they were doing a special programme on Sunderland gaining promotion and they wanted a message of goodwill."

"I bet you were impressed."

"I'll say I was."

"What did you say?"

Alan smiled. "I suggested 'Howay, the lads' and spelt howay very carefully and added a bit of elaboration. She said she'd pass it on.

I could hardly believe it had happened. In fact this was just one of many similar experiences I seemed to be having every day of the trip."

"Give me a for instance."

"Well, I was in Biscotasing, Northern Ontario and stayed a couple of nights in a hunting lodge in bush territory. There was an outside toilet in a shed about thirty yards away. Ernie, an Ojibway Indian, who helped around the place, muttered: "There was a bear in the 'john' last night. I immediately developed a previously unknown medical syndrome called forty-eight hour constipation."

Glad Alan wasn't with us in the Yukon. We were told if we wanted to 'go' we just had to find a convenient tree. We were in a hunters camp, rife with roaming wild beasts. The 'lodge' was raised off the ground with a small, narrow walkway leading to the door. "To stop the bears paying you a visit."

Very comforting.

Alan said a young boy who thought he talked 'real funny.' and added, 'like somebody on television.' but he couldn't remember who. Suddenly in the middle of a conversation he triumphantly yelled, 'I know, I know. Everybody in the Sound of Music."

I lived for many years in Canada and the tales recounted by the old-timers are going in 'The Touchwood Trail' - as a quick foretaste I thought you might like the story about Mike who always wore a Davy-Crockett-style coonskin cap.

He and his companion Ernie were out deer hunting when a big male racoon jumped onto his head and tried to mate with his hat, while still attached to Mike's head!

"My God he was a determined lover," said Mike while recovering later in hospital.

The bizarre experience had left him with 30 stitches in his face. They'd even had to sew his left ear back on.

Needless to say, Mike only wore woollen hats after that.

To finish off with here's a conversation I had with my friend Alf Stephenson when he heard I was due to visit British Columbia. He asked me if I was going to the Rockies. "Yes," I told him. "Well," he said, "I've been told if you go into the woods it's highly likely you'll meet a grizzly bear, but don't worry, I've also been told they usually avoid contact with humans, but to let the bears know you're in the area, attach a small bell to your wrist, but if you see bear droppings you have to leave the area at once."

"But how will I know if they're bear droppings?" I asked. Rather sensibly I thought.

"Easy," he replied, "If they're grizzly's, they'll be full of little bells."

CARIBBEAN

An inter-island flight around the Caribbean, is a breathtaking spectacle. Islands appear below as tiny azure jewels in a melting pot of colour. Tongues of spray can be seen leaping and dancing like ballerina's in perpetual motion. Fishing boats, cargo boats, slow boats, fast boats all floating in a myriad of hues as the sea flaunts its ebullient waters - Breathtaking!

The supermodel and singer, ***Caprice***, says: "The Caribbean is my ideal holiday destination because I just love somewhere hot and where there aren't too many people, also where the food is great. It has all of those, so they're the reasons I absolutely adore it."

Cricket supremo ***Denis Compton*** would never go away during the cricket season. "Also," said his wife Christine, "We have four cats which proves a problem as we don't like leaving them. On holiday we like to put our feet up and maybe Denis will nip to a golf club. But we did have a wonderful holiday in the Caribbean with our daughter. Denis played cricket with her constantly, but she wasn't impressed as he likes to bat and Charlotte nearly always has to bowl."

Kuoni Travel invited six travel agents to join them on an island hopping tour of the Caribbean. I was one of the lucky ones.

We visited Antigua, Barbados, Martinique, Mustique, St. Lucia and Trinidad - all in eight days!

We would arrive at out destination in the early evening and be welcomed at the airport with a cool drink. A short coach ride to our host hotel and another cooling drink. After a quick wash and brush up we would be taken on a tour of the hotel and grounds, followed by dinner, usually hosted by the tourist board - more liquid refreshment and bed about 1am. 6.30am an alarm call would jangle us into consciousness. Half-awake bodies would assemble in the foyer for a coach trip to another hotel for breakfast, after the obligatory inspection of the hotel and grounds. 9.30am and we'd be on our way again, another hotel, more hospitality, another inspection. Eleven and we'd be making our rounds of yet another hotel, after drinks of course. Lunch was usually at our fourth hotel - imbibing actively encouraged - but I'm sure you understand that walking around grounds in 90 degree heat made it imperative, nay essential, that we keep up our body fluids.

Late afternoon another internal Liat flight, another drink, another island, another drink, another hotel, another drink........

A hectic agenda, but never a dull moment.

Take BARBADOS for instance, the first island on our itinerary.

We were comfortably sat in a mini-bus heading for our hotel, when an agent from Cardiff took a deep breath and exclaimed: "This is wonderful. I love the smell of the Caribbean."

She was right. The bus was on fire! Flames burst through the floor as the last passenger spilled onto the sidewalk. Talk about luck. We'd come to a smoking halt right outside the fire station. It was doused in seconds. They didn't even have time to don their hats. We stood cheering and then would you believe the driver got back in and tried to start it up again. We cheered even louder. Well you had to give him 12 out 10 for trying.

The fire brigade offered us their hospitality. They said it was a special Barbadian fruit punch. It was definitely a punch, but fruit?! After an hour none of us cared if a donkey cart had come along to pick us up. Actually it was two cars and a truck - for the luggage - that did turn up to collect us. But both cars broke down the minute we got into them. More rousing cheers, so six intrepid explorers, sorry, travel agents, decided it would be much more fun to travel in the back of the truck. Much to the consternation of our Barbadian guide.

You should have seen the face of the hotel manager when we arrived at the entrance of his five-star establishment. (see Bahamas and John Prescott story.)

We all climbed over the tailboard of the truck, well all except Ernie who had collapsed in a smelly, comatose heap among the luggage.

So there we were unwashed, unashamed and ever so slightly inebriated.(and me a tee-totaller)

It was now 2.15am and we'd been travelling for over twenty-four hours and we were told we had to be up bright eyed and bushy tailed in three and-a-half hours.

Breakfast. Uugghh!! was taken in another hotel at 7.15.

Three hotels later, management asked if we'd take part in a goat race on the beach. Three gallant souls - all girls - accepted the challenge.

You don't actually race goats. Each contestant is allocated a goat, on a leash and you run with it. Everyone was ordered to "hang on whatever happens." Further along the beach a young man started calling the goats. Wham! They took off like exorcet missiles, but not necessarily in the same direction or at the same time. Two who were obviously old hands at this, refused to budge an inch and just gave condescending looks to their handlers. Other contestants just hung on grimly as their animals sped off. The first body to the shouting male was the winner. But only with a goat!

Two did make it, but one wouldn't stop and a pantomime ensued while various members of staff tried to head it off, with screaming female still attached!

My lasting memory was Rosalie being pulled along by the Red Rum of the goat world, when he/she abruptly stopped. Rosalie didn't! Got the picture? I usually have my camera at the ready, but on this occasion I was laughing so much I missed the vital moment.

Have you ever tried your hand at snorkelling? You enter a world of unblemished radiance. In the dancing light you can see a kaleidoscope of iridescent fish perform a magical ballet. It's a world of beauty and wonderment.

I remember ***Billy Connolly*** recalling his experiences in Barbados. He said he was gently swimming in the warm crystal waters of the Caribbean, luxuriating in the sight of shoals of gaudy and spectacular fish gliding and darting around his ringside seat. "I'd only recently seen the film 'Jaws'," he said "and suddenly I saw the shoal below me, speed away in a great surge. Now I think, do they know something I don't know, so I look nervously around. Not a bloody fish in sight. I'm looking everywhere and as I tread water, I spy this big black thing about three feet behind me in the water. It seems to be moving pretty fast. I'm screaming, 'It's a shark, it's a shark and real panic sets in. As you can imagine! I start threshing my way to the shore, which quite suddenly appears to be at least a mile away. Then my mind puts into focus what my eyes had actually seen. My flippers!! But too late," he said, "I'd already suffered a mild coronary."

There is a problem endemic in hot countries. They all have a lot of very large creepy crawlies. Cockroaches are everywhere and although I didn't see too many, the one's I did see were disguised as bullfrogs. God they were big! "They not hurt you Missy," said a young Barbadian. "But you keep shoe handy to splat him."

The thought of splattering something big enough to eat you for breakfast, could quite put you off travelling for life.

An American entomologist at Florida University was quoted as saying: "Cockroaches make you feel miserable, not only for their ugliness, but for scientific reasons."

"And they can actually kill you. Just spotting them can cause anaphylactic shock, breathing difficulties, rapid heartbeat, falling blood pressure and heart failure."

There, that makes you feel better doesn't it?

I was telling ***Lionel Blair*** about my encounter with the monster from the deep and he told me he had the perfect solution.

"You have?"

"Oh, there's no splatting with shoes. My solution's not nearly as messy."

"Tell me more." I urged.

"Well it's like this Dorothea. These beasts usually come foraging at night, right?" I nodded. "Well all you do is wait 'till they're in the middle of the room, then switch all the lights on. They in turn will propel themselves at a fair rate of knots back to their nest or wherever cockroaches hang out. Then you switch off the light."

I was not impressed and told him. "Yes, but then they'll come back."

He gave me a cheeky grin. "No, honestly it works. Just keep doing it and you'll worry them to death!"

This will please a client of mine. She came into the shop one day and was telling me about the 'wildlife' she'd encountered on her visit to Spain: "Oohh, Dorothea," she shuddered, "It's not that they're insects, but they're foreign insects."

Oh, something else about cockroaches you might find interesting. In China this 'beast' is a delicacy. It can be marinated in wine for a day or two, or maybe you'd prefer just common old garden, deep fried cockroach. Or you can always add to the delicacy by smothering it in chocolate. But honestly you haven't lived till you've tried cockroach studded pancake, or my favourite, cockroach porridge. Och aye the noo!

On our return to the UK after our whirlwind island hopping adventure, we had to stay over one night in Barbados. As our flight arrived from St. Lucia, we filed through customs proudly wearing straw hats which had been purchased three hours earlier.

"Take off your hats."

We took them off.

"Now give them to me."

"But we want to wear them."

"NO.NO. NO. You cannot enter Barbados with plants."

"But they're hats, made of palm leaves."

"Exactly. Plants. They have to go in quarantine 'till you fly away again."

It took over half-an-hour to fill out numerous forms. We were told that we had to enter our hats in the 'live' column.

Just a tip, after your wonderful holiday in Barbados whatever check-in times have been advised, double it, and allow at least three for internal flights!

I speak with experience, believe me!

Scenario:

5.30pm arrive at airport - Half-an-hour early.

The desk is deserted, but a queue was already forming, but we decided to go for a coffee.

6.00 Official check-in time. We return for our flight to Antigua, which is due to depart at 7.30am. There we have to catch the connecting plane to Heathrow.

6.05 Check-in still deserted.

6.15 Still no sign of any staff.

6.30 A body approaches and sits at desk but does nothing.

6.40 Tannoy announcement. "Antigua flight delayed until 7.40pm"

We all heave a sigh of relief.

7.00pm and there were still six people in front of us, never mind the fifteen behind!

At the next desk all hell was letting loose.

"Miami flight gone," said a clerk, "so it's no use me taking your luggage." and off she went, leaving ten passengers in a queue who, like us had been shuffling forward very slowly, for over an hour.

7.20pm. We thought we'd be lucky if we made the flight at all, never mind the connecting flight to London - And our bloody hats were still in quarantine!

Malcolm went to a uniformed attendant and explained our dilemma. He said he would see what he could do.

7.30pm. We were still waiting to check-in.

No announcement had been made, so we assumed our flight was ready to wing its way to Antigua. Well they did say take-off 7.40pm.

7.38, we were checked in and luggage taken away.

"Run, run, run," shouted a young man.

We ran. Passport control loomed. There, all lined up on a desk were our straw hats ready for collection.

"Run, run, run." screamed the same young man, now almost hysterical, while racing ahead of us. We ran, hats now jauntily perched on our heads.

7.46, the plane took off. We were all convinced that in 8 minutes our luggage had not a cat in hell's chance of being loaded.

We arrived in Antigua and were rushed through the transit lounge in three minutes flat.

Now we knew our luggage wouldn't make it with us to London.

But oh ye of little faith. There it was waiting for us on the carousel. How they managed it we'll never even guess, but it put a delicious end to an astonishing and unforgettable experience.

BRITISH VIRGIN ISLANDS

One of my favourite places, although I did have a rather calamitous moment in an island called descriptively 'Bitter End.'

The previous day we'd visited the trendy West Indian hideaway of St Bartholomew. It boasts only a few hundred de-luxe hotel rooms, and about 200 five-star luxury villas, whose rentals start at over £5,000 per week - Don't all rush at once now.

The manager told us a lovely story about two of the famous stars who had recently visited the resort.

"*Mel Gibson* was playing Treasure Hunt with his children and he suddenly spotted *Richard Dreyfus* wearing the inscribed Rolex watch he'd buried only a few minutes earlier as the star prize for his kids to unearth. Mr Gibson said he couldn't say anything to him, as he'd claimed it as legitimate treasure trove."

Some of the other celebrities who flock to this exclusive and exotic island are, *Jane Fonda*, *Richard Gere*, *Cindy Crawford*, *Whitney Houston* and *Claudia Schiffer*. They are guaranteed privacy, probably the reason the late *Princess Diana* visited it with her two sons.

We spent only one night there as we still had another island to visit. A speedboat arrived and we were taken to 'The Bitter End Yachting Marina in Virgin Gorda.

The following day after lunch the owner asked me if I'd like to see the shark pen at the end of the jetty.

"Love to," I replied and off we sauntered. What I didn't know, was lurking half-way along the walkway was a two inch step. In the bright sunlight it merged perfectly with the wooden planking. I fell headlong, missing the shark pen by inches. I broke both my arms. My right arm was dangling temptingly in the water - God, I thought, I hope they've had their dinner. Standing nearby was *Richard Branson* and his children. His private island Necker is in the same waters and he is a frequent visitor to the myriad of marinas in the area.

He witnessed the accident and immediately offered his assistance. He had his mobile at the ready but as a guest of the Virgin Islands Tourist Board, they already had alerted the emergency services. There's a laugh! Not a nurse or doctor within twenty miles. I looked up, there was probably 30 million pounds worth of yachts bobbing in front of my eyes and it looked as if they couldn't muster a elastoplast between them and the owner of the island seemed more intent on asking the most bizarre and irrelevant questions.

As I lay there, surrounded by anxious faces, I noticed Katie, a member of our party, pushing her way forward. She'd skipped lunch, deciding instead to top up her suntan. She stood in front of me, resplendent in bikini and green sun block, which had bits of grass sticking to it. "You look like something out of Midsummer's Night's Dream," I told her. Robin who was kneeling beside my prostrate body muttered, "More like something out of Dad's Army."

Katie was not impressed, but a sudden commotion to our left heralded the arrival of the cavalry in the shape of a sky-blue speedboat.

I was carried on board, with Mr Branson hovering just in case. Well he had offered to fly me home on Virgin Airlines if required. They laid me out - not literally you understand - on a hard plastic seat. We set off for Beef Island like an exorcet missile, hitting the waves with sickening regularity. Each time my body thuddded back onto the seat, I was convinced the next time I would be dumped upon the floor.

"You very brave missy," said a young islander, as he desperately clung to the side - He was just showing off because he had two working arms! I smiled weakly. "Could you - bump, bump - "do me" - bump, bump - "a favour?"

He nodded enthusiastically.

"Could you, sort of hang onto my legs to stop them lolloping about?"

He looked bemused.

"Lollops?"

Ah, maybe now was not a good time to be giving lessons on Yorkshire slang.

"My legs, can you hang onto them, they're falling off."

I was going to add, with the rest of my body, but what the hell.

He clung on very manly and after twenty minutes, 'brave missy' was being lifted into an ambulance, which would transport me to the nearest hospital in Tortola. I guessed the roads might be a tad pot-holed when they strapped me in to the ambulance like an Egyptian mummy!

During the ride I had time to cogitate on the line of questioning the owner of Bitter End had subjected me to. Of course! She thought I would be suing her for every penny/cent she had. Upon reflection I could now probably be a very rich lady.

At the hospital there was just one Malaysian nurse and an admissions clerk, on duty. Obviously an x-ray was required, but they couldn't locate a radiographer. "He'll be on one of the other islands," they said airily.

We chatted pleasantly for about an hour, with me perched on an operating table. Suddenly the door opened and in strode a tall, rangy individual in shorts and floppy straw hat. It was the islands surgeon and he was English. He'd only popped in for some papers, so was more than a little surprised to see me sat twiddling my thumbs - Ah, maybe not!

He had a quick look and appeared concerned about my right wrist.

"I think it might need an operation." he told me.

I explained I was on a fairly high dose of medication - namely steroids. I saw him visibly blanche.

"Tell you what," he said, "I'll pot you up now, then when you get back to England, get them to have a look at it." Forty minutes later I was climbing into a car heading for a de-luxe hotel, in which the tourist board had arranged for me to stay. I was informed I could make as many calls home as necessary. I only needed one. To my son Adam, who lived in London, to ask him if he could collect me at Heathrow.

The following day I was picked up by a chauffeur driven car and taken to the small airport to catch an internal flight to Antigua and onward to Britain.

A wheelchair was waiting for me and all formalities waived. I felt like royalty, but it got better. When I was ushered on board the Caribbean Airways flight in Antigua, ahead of all the other waiting passengers, I was led to first class.

I was sharing the cabin with just one other passenger. None other than ***Lord Glenconner***, (Colin Tennant) who at the time owned the island of Mustique. I recognised him immediately. Well I don't meet many six-foot-five men, wearing a wide brimmed, straw hat and bearing a black, silver topped cane. He exuded elegance but he never even glanced my way, but when one of my friends ventured through to the hallowed portals of first class, she was ushered away, obviously his Lordship should not mix with the hoi poloi!

After about an hour he settled down, his feet encased in a pair of navy, leather monogrammed slippers and went to sleep, straw hat perched nonchalantly over his face.

When I landed, my son was waiting. The surgeon had advised me to go a hospital the minute I landed but I thought, what the hell, I'll be home in a few hours and it couldn't make that much difference, so we headed North down the M1. I popped in to see my husband and give him the good news, then Adam whisked me off to the Hull Royal Infirmary.

The pots were perfect and no operation was necessary.

I went to work two days after my return. I managed perfectly well, mind you going to the loo was more than a bit inconvenient.

The local paper ran a story on the incident and it was seen by the local ***M.P John Prescott***, who happened to be lunching at the Dorchester with ***Richard Branson*** the following day. He took the cutting with him to show Mr Branson, who wrote a get well message across the article and asked him to give it to me the next time he was in my company.

I thought you might be interested in details of Necker, the 74 acre island owned by Richard Branson
He bought it in 1979 for the princely sum of £200,000. I read that he has spent about £14 million developing it as an ultimate retreat. Many stars book the island as the perfect hideaway, including ***Phil Collins***, ***Richard Dryfuss***, ***Harrison Ford***, ***Steven Spielberg*** and the late ***Princess Diana***.

The house can cater for up to twenty guests.

It is built in the Balinese style, with all the furniture specially made from giant bamboo.

You have the services of a live-in chef to cater for your every whim.

There is a full size snooker table, countless tapes and records and over two hundred videos, all updated regularly and a library with all the best sellers. There's even a games chest catering for all ages. It includes such favourites as Snakes and Ladders and Trivial Pursuits.

It's available to anyone who has the were-with-all. But I wont spoil your dream...Let's just say that St. Bartholomew at £5,000 a week, is a snip as that includes the flights. Necker is more than that A DAY and does not include the trip to America. They're extra, but don't despair, they do provide a helicopter from New York to the island, also the use of speedboats and jet-skis while in residence. There that makes it sounds more appealing doesn't it?

While we're on the subject of owning your own hideaway, as I write this, an island owned by the late Scottish-American publishing millionaire, ***Malcolm Forbes***, is for sale.

For most of us it's a dream, but the likes of Mr Branson and Mr Forbes can afford to make heaven an earthly reality.

It was 1972, when the publisher bought Laucala, an island off Fiji, with 3,000 acres of tropical rain forest, palm groves and beaches. And according to his 'idyllic concept', he developed it into a private resort, with a luxury house and seven thatched holiday bungalows. It's now for sale, complete with village, occupied by 220 Fijians, a Twenties plantation house and a grassy airfield and it's a tempting £6.25 million. But don't get despondent, you can rent a chalet at £1,500 a week and that includes all meals.

You've got to admit, it's a snip.

JAMAICA

It is said that when you go to Cephalonia in the Greek Islands, every other tourist is lying back with a copy of Captain Corelli's Mandolin. It is now much the same with Jamaica and How Stella Got her Groove Back - except the locals are all reading it too.

The story goes that ***Terry McMillan*** was tempted to hop on a plane from California to a luxury beach hotel in Negril in 1995. It was the thought of guaranteed pleasure that did the trick.

She thought it might help her after getting a divorce and the pressures of raising a black male child on her own.

The book and subsequent film tell the story of Stella's romance with Winston, a hotel worker 22 years her junior.

I stayed in Negril when I visited this luxuriant island.

Even though poverty is prevalent everywhere, you can see children as young as three or four walking alone.

On Sundays, loud and joyful singing can be heard emanating from the churches. I saw immaculately dressed adults and children all carrying their shoes on their heads to keep them clean for the service.

Visit Rick's Cafe I was told, and being a dutiful girl I did. The entertainment included watching bodies plunge hundreds of feet from the cliff top - into the turquoise water of the Caribbean I hasten to add.

Talking to a young waiter - as one does - he said many Jamaican men find the white women very attractive, especially those over a size 14, and as soon as anyone size 18 plus hits the beach they are rapidly approached by young virile men who genuinely find them sexy.

The actress ***Lysette Anthony*** loved the island. "Even though we had an airport wait of over six hours before we set off on the nine-hour flight. We visited a wonderful market in Ocho Rios. There must have been over a hundred wooden shacks offering you a chance to look inside at their wares. Everybody cries out in a sing-song voice. 'Come pretty lady, you look inside. It free.' I ended up buying two wooden elephants, a carved head and a straw hat. Further along I was persuaded to have my hair braided by a young woman who insisted on showing me her stretch marks!"

"Did you succumb to the beach masseurs?"

"Oh yes. This really old woman brought out a chewed up palm leaf and rubbed all the sticky goo from it over my body. Ughh! I thought, this is awful, it's like having slime smeared over you, but it soon was absorbed by the skin and I felt invigorated. She was well over 60 but gave me a wonderful massage."

Lysette and her fiancee Luc. decided to hire a car. "The first they brought us never left the car park, the second had a leak."

I said they must have been taking lessons from the Maltese, but that's another story! Anyway it was third time lucky for Lysette. "Until," she said, "we were stopped by the police for speeding. We were doing 20mph! But the traffic cop would have none of it and insisted we were doing forty-six miles an hour. 'It's not allowed in a built up area.' he told us. She smiled. "The built-up area was two small houses, one on each side of the road. We argued and said we couldn't possibly be doing that speed, even if our speedometer was wrong. Surely it couldn't be that far out. Luc and I looked at each other and together said, 'Could it?!' Anyway we asked to see a demonstration on the next car that came along. It showed over fifty, but it was obvious they were driving well within the limit. With those pot-holes it was impossible to reach fifty! In exasperation the policeman pointed it at a nearby wall. It was doing nearly twenty. End of case.

"Oh, by the way," said Lysette. "Those roads are definitely not suitable for scooters."

She was asked if she would go back to Jamaica.

"What could be nicer than enjoying glorious weather on a beautiful island in the middle of an English winter. I'd certainly go back."

My second visit to the island was at the tail end of Hurricane Gilbert. All electricity and water was off, but the staff were not to be beaten. I went to the reception desk to ask if they knew what was happening with the water supplies. I was greeted with a huge grin and told, "You not worry Missy, you go back to room, we get you water."

True to their word, twenty minutes later a knock at my door and there stood Horatio with two buckets full of water. "I put this in bath Missy." "Can't you leave the buckets?" I asked. "Oh, no Missy, we need them." He tipped out the water and disappeared. The water smelt funny. I found out the staff was scooping the water from the pool with the only two buckets available. You had to admit, they were nothing if not resourceful.

In the grounds of my luxurious hotel, I noticed that all the palm trees had silver strips about a foot deep, wrapped around the trunks approximately five foot up. I asked the manager the reason.

"Oh, that's to stop the rats getting at your nuts."

I bet all the fellah's walk pretty briskly around that hotel!

By the way don't worry when you see men loitering on all the available walls brandishing machettes, I learned to my relief that they were only to cut the bush down - well that's what they told me!

While walking along, exploring the area outside the hotel, we came across a small market. At the time Ray smoked rather large cigars and while pottering around the stalls, we noticed three young men peering at us from around a small, brightly coloured, wooden shack. We smiled. They positively beamed, then pointed to Ray's cigar and danced around shouting "Oh, man, you big man!" Obviously very impressed by the size of Ray's smoke. As we left the market and were wandering slowly along the dusty road, Ray was accosted by a very old, wizened female, offering her wares. No not that, she was offering him some 'magic mushrooms.'

"They come from all over world for my mushrooms. I get you really good mushroom. You try?"

She looked and sounded like Bloody Mary, that character in South Pacific.

At the time we were completely naive and hadn't a clue what she was talking about or why Ray's cigar had caused such excitement.

When we got back to the safety of our hotel, I couldn't help but comment on our little escapade to a local.

He laughed loudly. Evidently the young men had thought Ray had been smoking 'waccy backy,' and 'magic mushrooms'? Well they do indeed come from all over the world to sample their delights, "but," he said, "they are also illegal and would knock your socks off."

Alan Plater visited the island on a fact finding tour for a forthcoming BBC documentary. He was taken on a ten-day tour by a couple of local guides - Carl, an actor and red-eyed Rastafarian and his cousin, who was an expert on banana cultivation. But let Alan continue: "They took us to places white people rarely go, including meeting with the council of Maroons who live in the interior of the island. One night we stayed in one of the top tourist hotels in Jamaica - close to ***Noel Coward's*** old pad - and the guys conducted us with so much laughter to what they assured us was 'a very special room.' Indeed it was. It had a circular bed. Shirley (Alan's wife) took a look and said: "That's fine but where's the mirrored ceiling?"

MARTINIQUE

On my island hopping adventure we visited the Museum of Volcanic Eruption and were being shown around by a very proud islander.

He pointed to a glass case filled with what appeared to be a pile of pale grey sand. "That very fine hashish, no?"

"Yes," we all agreed, trying not to look surprised, it was very fine indeed. It was some time later when we found out he was talking about volcanic *ashes.*

Also while taking a trip to the rain forests, the French speaking Martinique guide said to us: " If you find any mistakes in my English. Please pass on."

The following day we were flying out to St. Lucia, but when we went to check in there were only three seats available, even though they had been pre-booked three weeks previously.

Three of us 'volunteered' to catch the following flight, three hours later.

We all headed to a cafe for a spot of lunch. This was one of the more civilised Caribbean airport cafes.

I ordered a cheese salad and fresh orange juice. The price? the equivalent of £8.90. The other two ordered chips with everything. The cheapest came to £9.95. We waited over forty-five minutes before we were served. As the plates were being put in front of us an airline official came and asked if we were waiting for the St. Lucia flight. We admitted we were.

"Well you come now. Plane left."

"Yes," we said, "We know plane left, we're waiting for the next one."

"No, you not understand. Plane left. You must come quickly."

We hadn't a clue what he was talking about but he seemed pretty agitated so we followed him. Butties, chips and orange juice were flying all over the place - well at nine pounds a toss, we certainly weren't leaving them - We grabbed our belongings and followed the yelling man.

We were led at the speed of sound along corridors and eventually to passport control, who true to form insisted on checking every mosquito splat and watermark they came across. Our little man was getting impatient and shouting what we gathered were very unflattering remarks to his compatriots.

Next the x-ray machine. My camera bleeped. Well it would wouldn't it. It had to be inspected - very closely!

We continued going at what can only be described as 'hell for leather' and we hadn't a clue why.

We raced across the tarmac and up the steps into an aircraft.

"Do you think we're being kidnapped?" yelled Mike.

"Very likely," I yelled back.

As we were pushed into the cabin, there were all our party, sitting and wondering why the hell they hadn't taken off.

Good job we did take our lunch with us, it proved a welcome repast for us all.

MUSTIQUE

This is the island originally bought by its self-appointed patron, Colin "***Lord Glenconner***" Tennant, for £45,000 in 1958.

He gave a house to Princess Margaret - which we managed to have a sneaky look at - but he eventually ran out of money and was forced to move out, but his presence still lingers on.

He was described to me thus: "A cantankerous old windbag. The self appointed patron of the island."

"That's a bit mean," I said, "Surely he's not all bad?"

"Well no," they admitted, "I suppose you could also say he's an impossible ball of energy and frustration in white robes and a sad straw hat."

Although I saw little of this when I was returning to England, with Caribbean Airlines. As I've already mentioned he was the only other passenger frequenting first class and sat quietly on the opposite aisle to me. Casually leaning his silver topped cane beside him and slipping his 'sad straw hat' over his eyes - which he never took off once. He slept or read most of the flight home. I heard not a squeak from him, he appeared to be the model of decorum, not a sign of the rudeness and tantrums of which he was renowned.

For me Mustique is one of the most romantic places on earth. No night life, no shops or restaurants It's only three miles long and a mile-and-a-half wide and beloved of such stars as ***David Bowie*** and ***Mick Jagger***.

It's magical to wander along a deserted beach, picking your way among the huge, translucent conch shells, lying casually on the velvet sand.

When we landed, our hosts, the Cotton House Hotel, were waiting with fruit punches and a couple of jeeps to transport us to the hotel.

This is the only hotel on the island and we were delighted to find a film crew was also staying there with some page three girls, on a photo shoot.

My spacious room had a four-poster bed and a large fan softly cutting through the balmy air. I walked onto the balcony which overlooked lush, green, manicured lawns gently sloping down to beach of pink soft sand. All the paths were lined with pink, conch shells.

God, it's hard being a travel agent.

We had a few hours to spare, so we watched the filming for a while - Those girls were stunning - then the hotel said we could borrow their jeep if we wanted to pop down to Basil's Bar for lunch. (The only bar on the island.)

This is an evocative, magical place. A bamboo awning stretched over a small wooden platform which was surrounded by the crystal blue waters of the Caribbean. Moored, sleek, white yachts bobbed silently around this haven of tranquility.

The sunlight filtered through the awning of leaves, casting jewels of light across the floor. Unrivalled serenity - until you see the prices!

Charles, an agent from London exclaimed. "This is my Shangri-La, the drinks are on me." Now all Caribbean drinks are expensive and we thought Mustique would probably top the lot.

Most of us ordered fruit drinks or coke. The price for five drinks? Just over forty pounds!

It got worse. We asked to see a menu. Lobster was the equivalent of sixty pounds, chicken, forty and tuna, twenty-five. We decided to push the boat out and ordered a plate of chips! One between the five of us. Cost? Five pounds. We did have a bottle of ketchup thrown in, but no vinegar. Well, even Paradise has a price.

We then headed for a small secluded beach. Access was gained through a heavily wooded copse with dense foliage arching overhead, obliterating the rays of the afternoon sun. Hundreds of large - very large - crabs scurried across our path, just discernible in the deep shadows cast by the hanging boughs. They were soon lost in the undergrowth, but we weren't taking any chances and stayed in the jeep, until we hit the beach barefoot, it was soft and warm. We leapt and gamboled in absolute joy.

I've just remembered one client of mine who wouldn't have been impressed. She returned after a visit to Tunisia and said: "The beach was ridiculous, there was far too much sand on it." We paddled and splashed like children, then we noticed dozens of quite exquisite Conch shells lying discarded. Their pink translucency seemed to glow. It was breathtaking and stopped us in our tracks. Everyone excitedly chose a shell and placed them carefully in the jeep.

On our way back we discovered the islands church. Constructed entirely of bamboo.

Inside misty, angel beams filtered through latticed leaves, gently kissing the warm, wooden pews.

Silently we sat. Enchanted by the peace and tranquillity.

Paul and Maria slowly walked to the front and pretended to get married. The rest of the party paired off and 'did the deed.' All except me who was busy taking photographs of the happy couples.

I said I would let them all have a copy. All the men asked me not to send them to their homes, as they didn't want their partners to see them, while the girls couldn't wait to show them to anyone and everyone. What's that about men from Mars and women from Venus?

At the hotel, filming had finished, so after a shower we all congregated on the open-air balcony for dinner. Paradise indeed.

The following morning I was mooching around the small windmill in the gardens, which doubled as the souvenir shop, when I was asked if I'd heard the commotion the night before. I admitted I'd slept like a log.

I was told one of the hotel's assistants had been particularly helpful to one of the models who we'll call Belinda.

But let her tell the story: "We had all just retired to our rooms after dinner and I had just dozed off when I was aware of a large male figure framed in the doorway of my bungalow. I thought he was coming for me and I screamed out." She laughed. "I didn't know I could make so much noise. With that the man rushed forward, then suddenly the room seemed to be awash with armed guards and they took the intruder away."

"What had happened" said Belinda, "was a few members of our group had been teasing him and said that I'd taken a shine to him and if he played his cards right, nudge, nudge, wink, wink. Well the poor man had taken them a their word and decided to make a midnight visit. Anyway it all turned out all right. The crew were mortified when they found out how their teasing had backfired. I forgave them and insisted the young man helped with the rest of the shoot." She also said: "We're taking him with us to Basil's Bar when we finish."

I hope they paid!

The actor Nigel Havers describes the island "As pretty as a postcard and the one place you can get away from everyone because everyone else on the island is there for the same reason

ST. LUCIA

I remember the late Carry-On star, ***Kenneth Williams*** mentioning a card he'd received from the comic ***Stanley Baxter*** from this lush Caribbean island. Mr Williams said, "It showed a gnarled old fisherman sat by his boat on the seashore with his nets. His message read, 'I think I've overdone the make-up, but the petit-point is coming on a treat."

We arrived on the island ahead of our bags, which were due in 4/5/6/7 hours!

But the customs would not allow us to leave the terminal building - building! there's a laugh - until we'd claimed our luggage.

"Can't we go to our hotel and return when the flight arrives to claim the luggage?"

What a silly question.

The Kuoni rep. was seen pleading in the departure lounge. Well it was the same as the arrival hall really, it just had a broken old desk strategically placed half-way down. A St. Lucian, resplendant in uniform and tatty trainers, menacingly fingering a pistol, made sure we stayed where he commanded.

Chairs were numerous. Five plastic ones, obviously lifted from the local infants school, three high backed chairs, as used by the elderly - without any covering, just lumps of tatty sponge sticking out. A rocking chair, nailed to the floor, plus an arm chair with springs going through the seat and hanging like a disembowelled chicken from the base. Then I saw it. A splendid wicker work creation. It looked quite outstanding among its motley friends.

I sat. I leapt up again. As I'd relaxed into the bowels of the voluminous cane I noticed little black 'objects' walking all over it. God, I thought, that sun's stronger than I thought. Then I saw them leap into the air. I jumped - higher and quicker!

The armed, jobsworth wouldn't even let us go to the loo.

The rep. could still be seen flitting like a butterfly on speed between anyone with a uniform. She was not on a winning streak.

We, by now, had got out a pack of playing cards and were sitting on the floor playing three card brag. - a win and you got a sip of the only coke bottle between us.

An hour later the rep. shouted, "It's okay, they're letting you go, I can come back later to pick up the luggage."

We all rose, slowly, hardly daring to uncross our legs! But we made it without leaving one damp patch behind.

We all had to file past Mr Jobsworth while he scrutinised us and our passports as if we'd come to invade the island. As each was passed as suitable to visit his territory, there was an unsavoury scramble for the loos.

We were just climbing into the mini-bus, when we heard a plane. "We'd better wait, your cases might be on it," said Robin, the Kuoni rep.

They were. We were two hours late but they, were three hours early.

The following day we were taken on a tour of the island, interspersed with visits to several hotels. We were surprised to find not a single traffic light on the island.

Their 'busses' are a cross between a jeep, a truck and a mini-bus. Very sturdy, which is essential in their pot-holed roads. No bus-stops, people wait by the side of the road wherever is convenient for them and likewise when returning. You yell, he stops.

Sometimes the dialect is difficult to understand but once your ear gets accustomed to the lilt there's, 'no problem man.'

Our guide was a local who was a mine of information.

"You better not do anything wrong, 'cos we still got hanging here, but you English, you trying to get that repealed."

That's all right then.

She also told us, "It never rains in St. Lucia." Then with a wide grin announced: "You must all know why. Because everyone know we famous for our liquid sunshine."

As we were motoring along, the guide asked the driver to stop and told us all to look to our right. She informed us: "That's the breadfruit tree."

She was asked if they used the fruit.

"Oh, yes," replied the guide. "We use it like your Irish ones."

"Our Irish ones?" We were perplexed.

"Yes. We make ships with them."

We were even more puzzled. "Ships?"

"Yes, you know," replied the smiling girl. "Fish and ships."

She also went on to give us a piece of invaluable advice: "Never, ever ask a St. Lucian the way. He'll invariably pick out something live to guide you by. You know, something like.'When you come to the brown cow in the field, turn left and keep going 'till you get to the three goats. It's just past them."

She was quite easy to understand but when the islanders used Pigin English, now that was something else. Our guide was only too pleased to give us a quick lesson.

"What would you make of Apple belongs stink?" she asked. We hadn't a clue.

"Easy if you think about it," she said. "It means an onion."

Ah, now it was making sense.

"What about 'Gubmint catchem fellah?"

We shook our heads. "A policeman" she announced, then asked, "What about, grass belong face?"

We all shouted as one. "Whiskers."

While sitting on a beach - well we did have two hours to spare! - we were offered some sun hats, all woven with palm leaves while we waited.

They were all different and original. Mine had a bird of Paradise sitting on a long slender branch from the crown I've still got it twenty years on.

We were all collected and we made our way to the airport for our flight to Barbados.

This time we took off without mishap. In fact we took off twenty minutes early.

Little did we know the problems which lay ahead - all because of our .50p hats!

COOK ISLANDS

After ***Alan Plater*** had completed his three-month teaching stint in Australia, he said he'd like to return home via the Cook Islands, a destination he and his wife Shirley had always wanted to visit.

The flights and hotels were booked and an itinerary forwarded to them. After checking the details, they rang me say they thought I'd made a mistake.

"I think you've got one of the dates wrong," said Alan.

I got his file out. "Right, which date are we looking at?"

"The day we arrive. You've got us landing in Raratonga a day before we take off from Auckland."

I laughed. Not my error after all. "That's because you cross the International date Line."

He was delighted. "That's wonderful. I'll be a day younger."

He was more than a little impressed in the fact he was catching himself up.

When they returned they both agreed that it was probably the loveliest place they have ever visited.

Alan explained: "It's a genuine tropical paradise. The islanders tell you that there is nothing on the island that will hurt you. On a bus tour round the island we were shown a modest single-storey structure that looked like a cricket pavilion and were told: that is our Parliament building.

There was a notice on our bedroom saying.'Do not offer tips to our staff as it offends their dignity.'

I once fell foul of the tipping aspect. I needed a wheelchair in Java - you don't want to know! - and a young man in his late teens, was escorting me while we waited for our flight to Bali. Nothing had been too much trouble. I found out he was the only one working out of a family of nine. When it was time to leave, I offered him all the local currency I had, about £2.00, which was four days pay to him. He was mortified and refused point blank to accept it. I felt dreadful. Nobody had warned me. I had obviously 'offended his dignity'.

As Alan said, "The problem as ever is that places like that are easily ruined by people like us."

CORSICA

I joined a host of media bodies and travel agents on a trip to Corsica.

We had all been invited on the inaugural flight to the island.

Off we sped in great anticipation as we'd been promised a splendid reception when we landed.

We all filed off the aircraft laughing and joking having all imbibed freely on the flight over.

Suddenly a representative of the airline approached us. "Sorry folks, but I'm afraid there's no time for jollity, you have to re-board immediately."

We had managed four minutes on French soil before being hustled back into our seats.

Well at least we had a few hours to sample the delights of airline food and wine and champagne and wine and liqueurs and champagne and... Need I go on?

Agony aunt, ***Claire Raynor*** was holidaying in the island and couldn't find a hairdryer in the room, so decided to go down to reception with her head wrapped in a towel. As she explained, "I did that because I couldn't for the life of me remember what the word for hairdryer was, so when I arrived at the desk and asked for 'vent chaud,' I thought this was a very good description of what a hairdryer provides - hot air. What I didn't know, of course, was that in French that phrase means a hot fart! They eventually worked out what it was I needed and managed to provide it, and I became a very popular guest at the hotel because I spoke French so amusingly!"

CRUISING

Holidays have proved a pain for actress ***Liz Dawn***, when she's taking a break from playing Coronation Street character Vera Duckworth.

"Twice I've put my back out when I've been away," said Liz.

"The first time was with the grandchildren on the Norfolk Broads then I did an encore on a fortnights Caribbean cruise.

"I spent a week in bed in our cabin and only saw six islands through a porthole. As I lay there, I'd say, 'Is that Guadaloupe?"

Libby Purves, columnist for the magazine Woman and Home remembers the time, in childhood, she came home from the Far East on a cargo ship, one of the last mailships. "I inhaled the smells of Zanzibar, Mombassa and Cairo and watched as the cargoes swung aboard in huge nets. I sat in a deck chair gazing at seabirds swirling and thinking this way of travel would never end." As Libby says, "Aeroplanes are very handy but sometimes the heartless briskness of it all makes me long for time and ships."

Another story from ***Claire Raynor***. She said she was lecturing on a QE2 cruise and had requested a separate dining table. "It was perfect, a little table tucked right away," said her husband Des. "But sure enough, as soon as we raised our soup spoons to our lips, a woman marched over, saying,'Claire, I'm so glad you're on board, I've got this terrible problem...!'

"Why," asked her husband, "do people think they own her?"

Sarah Kennedy often regales her early morning listeners with tales told to her by her friend Rupert, a steward on board a cruise liner.

Typical story: "Excuse me steward but can you tell me when the midnight buffet is served?"

She also recounted the time a ship was cruising the Mediterranean and the passengers were booking for their shore excursions.

"An American couple had booked every trip available - except one -'Were not sure about that one,' they told the girl, "We don't really like theme parks."

"The theme park in question?" asked Sarah, "Gibraltar!"

But Rupert's not the only one to have had a few odd questions thrown at him.

One afternoon I'd just boarded the P & O's Oriana, on its maiden voyage to the Norwegian Fjords. An elderly lady, looking rather confused asked me: "Excuse me, but can you tell me if these stairs go up as well as down?"

And here's three from clients in the travel agency.

"We're going on a Greek islands cruise. Will there be water all around the islands?"

"Do you think we could ask for afternoon tea in the morning?"

And my favourite: "Do the crew sleep on board?"

The renowned artist ***Aude Herail Jager*** was asked if her ship went down off a desert island and she was on her own for some considerable time before being rescued, what she would miss most about civilisation - Answer: "The idea of travel; and immersing myself in otherness. The idea of popping into a plane under a dull sky and popping out of it and hearing a ukulele."

There was a slight pause before she was asked: "What would be the first luxury you would indulge in on your return?"

"To be airlifted in an old-fashioned air balloon and travel home in a glider - not to be confused with a water glide! A long silent flight through the sky would bridge my experience of the island and civilisation."

Did you understand a word? Apart from the fact that she had obviously never been on a glider. My first boss, Brian MacFadden was a glider nut and he invited me and the family to Pocklington airfield to experience a flight. When we eventually became airborne I was acutely aware of the horrendous noise the wind made as the machine cut through the air. It would be anything but a quiet and peaceful return for Ms Jager.

I remember one client in Hull who had been on a cruise to the Canary Islands and on the second day she inadvertently flushed her teeth down the loo.

She told me: "The captain said he would flush out the bilge tank to see if he could find them, but I didn't fancy that, so I managed without them, but I didn't smile a lot."

Still on teeth, Mrs Browne from Cottingham lost her bottom set of dentures just before she was due to set out for Southampton.

"I can't possibly go now," she wailed to a friend.

"Nonsense," said her friend. "Haven't you got an old set somewhere?"

"Of course I haven't. Don't be so stupid." Mrs Browne started to cry.

"I know," said her friend. "Let's see if we can borrow some."

"I'm not wearing somebody else's teeth."

"If you don't, you'll lose all your money."

"Oh, God, I never thought of that. Mable next door wears dentures, wonder if they'd fit me?"

"Then what's she going to do for two weeks?"

"Oh, they're not hers as such. She's got a jar full of false teeth."

She duly went next door and surprise, surprise found a pair that fitted - sort of!

"I'll wear them now, so I can get used to them," she told her friend.

Slightly more happy, she went round the house turning off the gas and electricity. Last thing, she went to empty the rubbish into the bin and yes, you've guessed it, there nestling among the potato peelings and egg shells, was a set of false teeth. Owner was happily reunited with her property and everyone lived happily ever after.

CYPRUS

P*eter Adamson*, a Radio Humberside presenter told the listeners on his morning phone-in about someone he'd recently met on holiday. "They were wandering along looking for a suitable place to have lunch. As many of us do, they looked through the window first. The first one looked a bit scruffy, the second was full, but the third seemed just right. They opened the door and seated themselves at a circular table covered with an immaculate lace tablecloth. They ordered orange juice, which was brought immediately. "Could we have a menu please?" they asked the elderly lady who was hovering nearby. In halting English she said, "No, I live here." The embarrassed couple quickly rose and apologised profusely, offering to pay for the juice. He did go on to wonder, "What if that had happened in England. Just imagine, there you are..." he started his irrepressible giggle but continued, "having a few quiet minutes and a casually dressed couple walks through the door, plonks themselves at your table and ask for a drink." He giggled again and asked. "Come on now, how many of you wouldn't do the same thing?"

Aphrodite, The Goddess of love and beauty, is said to have been born of the 'soft sea foam off an outcrop of rock near to Paphos. The legend inspired an Italian poet, Aristo, to name a pool, north of Paphos, the Fontana Amorosa, or the Fountain of Love. It is said that all who drink the waters will fall in love - forever.

I wonder if that's what ***Richard Burton*** and ***Elizabeth Taylor*** did when they visited the island to film Cleopatra.

Mr Burton made headlines throughout the world when he gave an enormous diamond to Elizabeth during the filming, but the real Mark Antony, back in 36BC, presented the femme fatale of Egypt with an even more extravagant gift. The entire island of Cyprus, because, they say, of its reputation for excellent wines

In fact the late ***Kenneth Williams*** told me he'd always wanted to visit the island after he'd read about its reputation for fine wines and also its history and cuisine.

"But when I arrived it was pouring down with rain and we had a horrendous journey from the airport. The taxi-driver played incoherent pop gibberish and to make it worse it was foreign gibberish at 1000 decibels. When we arrived at the hotel, it got worse, the whole area was littered with building materials and giant slumbering bulldozers. What I didn't realise was, they were only quiet because of the torrential downpour. The peace was shattered at 7.30am the following morning when they commenced their work."

He shuddered. "I'll never go back there," he announced imperiously.

Denise Welch, that no-nonsense Natalie from Coronation Street, says her favourite place is Cyprus.

"These days I'm fortunate enough to be able to take the whole family on holiday. My sister's husband Peter is Greek, so his family and mine often meet up in Cyprus. I've been to many exotic locations which I loved, but put me on a lounger, rub in some sun cream, surround me with family and I'm in heaven."

EGYPT

Travel presenter, ***Mary Nightingale***, was in the country for the Wish You were here...? programme.

"I was amazed by the sight of the pyramids and I just couldn't understand why the cameraman wasn't as excited as me until he told me it was his seventh visit to film them! I never want to reach that position where I'm just visiting places and feeling as if I'm going over the same old ground again and again."

I have some wonderful stories about Egypt, including falling for the charms of a dark eyed, smoothie in a pristine white suit who led me astray, but I'll leave that for the next travel extravaganza.

FAR EAST

D*avid Janson* is familiar to most television viewers. He has a varied repertoire from Hamlet to pantomime. Television appearances includes. The Newcomers, Get Some In, Give Us A Clue, Brush Strokes, Eastenders and Ever Decreasing Circles.

He has a daughter called Ciarai.

I met David when he was touring in that extremely comedic play Watching, which was turned into a hugely successful television series.

David has toured extensively in the Far and Middle East. He says: "Singapore Airport is almost a second home to me. No matter where we were destined it seemed we had to transit Changi, the city's airport. Nine hours was the longest we ever had to wait there, but I never get bored. It's all that kaleidoscope of nationalities that pass through airports. Absolutely fascinating." He smiled. "I've got a confession though," he said. "We were nearly always travelling first or club class and that certainly smoothes away most of the nightmares associated with long distance travel."

"I know how you feel," I told him. " I've often been expected to attend a civic function only hours after arriving at my destination, so no time for the dreaded jet-lag."

"Frazzled is the word," said David. "Ours can be even worse, as we sometimes have to perform to an expectant audience with hardly any rest. On one journey we'd encountered delay after delay all along the way. It took us three days. We were only two days late! but we found a press reception had been arranged two hours after we'd checked into our hotel, also we were expected to be bright eyed and bushy tailed for the evenings performance. We managed. Just."

I was full of admiration and told him about a similar incident when I had been invited along with 14 other agents to a travel shindig in Bali. All the local dignitaries were assembled to welcome us.

We had only an hour-and-a-half to shower and change after twenty eight hours travelling, with only cat-naps throughout the journey.

It was very hot and humid, giving a sort of euphoric feeling. I can vividly remember trying to put my brain into overdrive but the gear stick was stuck very firmly in neutral.

I managed the reception reasonably well, but when we sat down to dinner, I could feel my head sagging lower and lower. Concentration was nil. "Ah," I thought, a quick splash of cold water is what you want my girl, so I excused myself and headed for the ladies. I splashed and splashed and splashed again, but still felt groggy. While I was there I thought I might as well make use of the facilities.

I went into a cubicle and sat down. Need I go into details? I fell asleep! Only someone knocking on the door twenty minutes later, brought me back to consciousness. Feeling better, I was not. That nap was fatal. It made me feel even worse. It took me about four days to recuperate. But I was only trolling around hotels and beauty spots, whereas David Janson and the theatre company, were exhausted but were still were expected to give scintillating performances to a packed theatre.

I asked David what happened if someone got the runs. "They have to soldier on," he said "But it's a near thing sometimes. We once had a lady cast member who was really quite ill, but she had to carry on for five nights, sleeping most of the day, that's when she wasn't sat on the loo!"

"Oh, I've just remembered another incident" he said, "***Leslie Phillips*** and his wife were in one production, when his wife fell down some steps, twisting her ankle really badly and bruising her thigh. It was amazing to watch her hobbling very painfully throughout the day, but with that Dr Magic, called adrenaline, which seems to surge through the veins when a stage entrance is about to be made, she was able to step on stage without a hint of a limp, but as soon as soon as she reached the dressing room, wallop, it all came back."

FRANCE

As I told you, I first met ***Paul Daniels*** on Australia's Gold Coast. But I later met him while he was performing at the Westfield Country Club, just outside Hull.

He gave me the eeekk! of the week.

He asked me: "Why does a Frenchman have only one boiled egg for his breakfast?"

"I don't know Paul, why does a Frenchman only have one boiled egg for breakfast?"

"Because ... Unoef is unoeuf!!"

Celebrity chef ***Jamie Oliver*** says he vividly remembers his first skiing trip with school but particularly the breakfasts.

"We went to France," said Jamie, "and one of the things I learned was the continental breakfast actually meant stale bread and disgusting jam. And on top of that we were expected to ski for five hours!"

CANNES

I had a wonderful week in this plush resort. It is usually packed with people no matter time of year you descend to their golden beaches and swish cafes. It is French chic at its highest.

I stayed in the Hotel Martinez, right on the front and I was delighted when I found they served afternoon teas and yes, you could have delicious home-made scones with jam - at a price!

While staying in the resort I was invited to a very posh do. Best bib and tucker was definitely the order of the day.

I looked out of my hotel window on the day in question and it was bucketing down.

Limousines had been laid on to collect all the guests, as the evening was to be held in the grounds of a chateau deep in the heart of the French countryside.

Two huge marquees had been erected with awnings across the entrance. Girls in flamboyant costumes and young men bearing flaming torches, were lined either side to greet the guests.

They were soaked. Hair straggling down their backs and wet faces illuminated by blazing, or should I say fizzling torches which were intended to form a triumphal arch, and the red carpet, which had been laid up to the entrance, was a squelching, soggy mess.

We were rushed into marquee number one and were delighted when we saw boarding had been placed under all the tables. At least it stopped our feet freezing at the end of our legs! What a stupid thing to say! They'd hardly be at the top would they?

The meal was superb and we had nothing but admiration for the sterling efforts of the waiters who'd had to battle through the monsoon, transporting the food to us.

After the pre-requisite speeches we were asked to adjourn to the next marquee, where surprise entertainment was waiting.

Easier said than done. Dresses were hoisted to knicker level - and above - trousers tucked into socks and inadequate umbrellas were being waved in a flurry as everyone tried to manoeuvre through what had now become a quagmire.

Seating had been arranged in a semi-circle of chairs - on grass! - Great lakes of water were forming in the folds above our heads, bringing the ceiling of the marquee dangerously close to our coiffered craniums.

The fanfare sounded. Our surprise guest made his entrance. It was none other than the dishy French singer ***Sasha Distel.***

He perched precariously on a small stool and with only his guitar as accompaniment started to serenade us. Well I think he was serenading us, we saw his lips moving, but the bombardment on the fabric of the tent was so fierce we could hardly hear a word. But he twinkled beautifully!

Then we noticed eyes were beginning to swivel towards the fold above Mr Distel's head. It was bulging with ice-cold rainwater, forming a huge hammock and threatening to flood over our distinguished guest.

One of the agents in the front row had a brainwave and with an umbrella started to poke at the offending balloon of water. It worked - well sort of - It sloshed crazily from above Sasha Distel, only to turn into a mini tidalwave and deposit itself over a diner sitting unconcernedly, twenty feet away.

He got a huge cheer, including one from Mr Distel as it discharged itself all over the unsuspecting man.

He was led away to clean up and the entertainment continued. The loudspeakers had been adjusted to compete with the elements outside and Mr Distel continued - It could only be ... Raindrops Keep Falling On Your Head, couldn't it? That got the biggest cheer of the evening. But I have to say. Sasha, you were wonderful, but even you must admit it was a bit of a no contest, but we all gave you 12 out of ten for trying.

DORDOGNE

Rolf Harris and his wife hired a villa in this picturesque part of France.

"I absolutely loved it," said Rolf. "I felt so relaxed and secure. I did quite a bit of painting and wandered around the markets. We used to buy freshly baked bread every morning. It was wonderful. Definitely something to be recommended."

Also the actress ***Gayle Hunnicut*** with journalist husband Simon Jenkins spent the summer in the Dordogne, on what Gayle called, "A bucket-and-spade holiday. But we stayed with friends in a magnificent chateau. It was a bit like a house party with eight adults and numerous children. Our summer holidays with all the family are very important to us and we love this area. It has everything."

NICE

The novelist ***Deborah Moggach***, explained. "We'd planned a luxurious holiday in that lovely resort, but the minute we arrived my husband did his back in and spent the whole week lying flat on the floor while I fed him croque monsieurs from a local cafe."

Fashion designer, ***Betty Jackson*** thought it would be a good idea for the family to go by train.

"The kids thought it exciting but my husband worried about thieves breaking into the berth so he barricaded us in, making sure no-one could enter. The train set off for Marseilles, and we fell asleep. Next morning we woke to find we were in a siding near Marseilles station. We'd overslept and the guards had assumed our was a locked empty berth. We bought an alarm clock for the return journey."

Travelling by train to the South of France is a delight. Breakfast was delivered to my 'car'. The pillows were plumped behind my head, then my 'man' placed a tray on my lap, opened the curtains and wished me 'bon apetite.'

Dawn had just broken and it was a complete joy to sit enjoying hot croissants and coffee while the stunning countryside flashed by.

Trains are a also delightful way to travel inland with its

untamed beauty and medieval villages perched on wooded hills. My favourite has to be a local train which shuttles amiably back and forth along the French coastline. Eventually arriving at Monte Carlo, but you can pop on and off as frequently as you like.

Evenings are particularly evocative. I would wander along the Promenade des Anglais, the air balmy with the smell of Umbrella pine and lights twinkling along the coastline like a million fireflies. Just one setback. I found some of the prices astronomical. I spotted a pair of men's wyncyette pyjamas on display in a shop. Wyncyette pyjamas! The temperature was in the 90's'! Then I saw the price. £245, and that was in 1987!

PARIS

One time star of Emmerdale, actress ***Jean Rogers*** decided to visit Paris for a romantic week-end.

"We arrived at Charles de Gaulle airport and it took nearly an hour to persuade a taxi to stop." said Jean. "When one finally did, he heard our British accents, muttered something about far too busy to drive tourists and shot off."

"How did you get to your hotel?" I asked.

"Phil., my husband, decided we should brave the Metro. We found it quite easy. The system tells you which direction you're going in. We used it all the time after that. We found it cheap and safe."

"Did you see everything you wanted?"

"Not really, you need two or three weeks to see everything."

"What did you enjoy the most?"

"Probably the fact that everywhere we looked couples were holding hands. It was so romantic." She went on. "On the last day we were having a quick kiss and a young man nearby said to Phil. "You lucky man, she very pretty. What you call English crumpet."

"It quite made our holiday."

Eric Knowles, the antique expert, loves Paris, and said: "For something really different, go for a meal in the Gare du Nord Railway station's restaurant. The interior is spectacular," said Eric, "But also you'll be served some gastronomic delights."

Something else he suggested was to take a side trip to Giverny to see Monet's garden. "But," he advised, "Go either very early or very late or you'll have to join a very, very long queue."

It's spectacular. Did you know that the Japanese bridge, water lilies and colourful beds were planted to reflect an artist's palette?

GREAT BRITAIN

B*ernie Clifton* admits Britain is his favourite holiday destination. "I've worked all the over the world," he told me, "but I love the variety in our country. You don't have to worry so much about the effects of the sun, meaning people can relax and get about more."

"I believe," he said, "that this should be used to promote and encourage people to stay in Britain. There's no-where like it."

The author and columnist ***Peter Hitchins*** admitted his childhood holidays were usually spent in a cove in South Devon or a seafront village on the Isle of Wight.

"I remember one really exotic year we had a fortnight in the Channel islands, reached in those days on a Douglas Dakota and I really loved them."

He carried on, "I don't think I'd enjoy them now, partly because the places have changed beyond recall, but also because I have been spoiled by the new freedom to travel. I can't make up my mind whether it is a pity or not, but sometimes watching the captive crowds slumped around holiday airports like defeated armies, I wonder if we have gained that much."

ENGLAND

"Globe-trotting is all very well, but ignore England at your peril, especially my beloved North." says ***Alan Plater.*** "The best cricket beaches in the country can be found at Filey and - speaking as a lifelong Hull City fan and therefore an expert - the roughest game of football I ever saw was on the beach at Scarborough between two teams of young miners from South Yorkshire. It was a classic case of never mind the ball, let's get on with the game.

Moving further North, the most beautiful building in the world is Durham Cathedral, and the most beautiful county in the land is Northumberland. Don't spread this around or it'll be ruined within ten years."

Alan continues in a nostalgic mode.

"Of all the holidays in a long life, the ones I look back on with the greatest love were those of childhood. I was born in Jarrow, and the family moved to Hull in 1938. For the next fifteen years or so, our holidays would consist of going back to Tyneside.

When I was a kid in primary school, people would say: where are you going for your holidays? I would say: Jarrow, and I couldn't understand why they laughed. What they couldn't know was that my grandparents spoiled me rotten.

My grandfather, a former steelworker, worked nights at the tube works and therefore was available through the day to take me out on great adventures. As far as I was concerned, that was the whole point of the shift system.

The adventures included going to the park to watch men playing bowls, walking to the river to see the ships, stopping on the way back to look at fire engines and again at Miss Pattison's ice cream shop - this at a time when ice cream was made in the back room in a tub, instead of by the cubic mile at Hemel Hempstead. We were like the old lags in Last of the Summer Wine, wandering around, getting up to harmless mischief. Another joy was going with my Uncle Harry to the level crossing because he knew the man who ran the signal box. There was a big stove and I used to 'help' pull the mighty levers that signalled the coal trains through.

I'm sure many of you will agree, there's nothing like a bit of nostalgia to bring tears to the eyes and I the guarantee the memories will come flooding back.

Travel agents are bombarded by information on new hotels, flights or destinations and you would not believe the hyperbole, press releases ooze, so I found it a refreshing change, during the reign of ***Margaret Thatcher***, to read the following from a hotel in Plymouth.

"Amidst much secrecy and all having been thoroughly searched and interfered with we were able to witness the arrival of our Prime Minister.

She had been very busy previously, visiting our local hospital. She looked absolutely super, with not a hair out of place.

She shook hands with the general manager and commented on how lovely our hotel was.

An hour later having met some party workers, she was off again and heading for Plymouth airport enroute for London.

It was all over so quickly - for once boring Monday had turned into a really exciting day. Now all the staff and police - they even had sniffer dogs! - could heave a great sigh of relief and return to their normal hum-drum activity."

I decided it must have been the 'interfered with' bit that really made their day, or was it those sniffer dogs pushing their noses into all those important little places that brought a rosy hue to the cheeks. It couldn't possible have been the presence of Margaret Thatcher...Could it?

Christopher Beeny had been relating a sorry tale about his visit to Madrid - but I'll tell you about that later - when he went on to tell me about a friend in Essex.

It's got nothing to do with holidays but I thought you might like it.

"It was Sunday and my friend had a leisurely breakfast and as usual went to take his dog for a walk along the leafy lanes near his home. He was wandering along slowly, enjoying the sights and sounds of the typical English countryside. He came to an unmanned level crossing, this time the gates were closed, awaiting the imminent arrival of the train. A car had already stopped and was patiently waiting when there was a screech of brakes as another car came hurtling around the corner, wheels locked in a blue mist as the driver struggled to stop. He didn't. Crash, bang, wallop, straight into the back of the stationary Cortina.

My friend hurriedly tied the leash of his dog to the small reflectors on the crossing gate while he went to see if anyone was hurt.

The train thundered by, unheard by the occupants of the two cars, who by now were arguing furiously. No-one had been injured but both bumpers were looking a little the worse for wear. Suddenly everyone was aware of a whimpering sound, so they all turned and there suspended twenty feet above the ground was my friends pooch. The poor thing had been taken upward by the gate as it had lifted to allow traffic to continue.

The cars were forgotten as they all congregated below the animal, making what they thought were soothing noises.

It was dangling well above anyones reach, so the Cortina edged towards the barrier and the tallest stood on the roof to try and reach the wriggling terrier, but to no avail. A hurried phone call to the emergency box of British rail and the they were able to lower the offending barrier and the small dog appeared none the worse for his ordeal."

Christopher smiled and told me. "All the time he was telling me about his pet I couldn't help but wonder what would have happened if he'd owned a Great Dane."

The actor ***Nicholas Lyndhurst*** is afraid of tall buildings and said he once was persuaded to visit the Post Office Tower in London. "At first I couldn't get out of the lift," he said - and I point blank refused to look out of the windows."

Actress and model, ***Jilly Cooper*** remembers going to Cornwall as a child. "I promptly fell in love with it. I made lots of friends and did all the things that kids do on holiday, like play leap-frog and eat huge ice-creams. It was great - and I even loved swimming in the freezing cold sea!"

Simon Williams, remembered for his portrayal of Major Bellamy in Upstairs, Downstairs. He has also written plays and novels.

"I was appearing in a play in the West End, but the family wanted a holiday so my wife Lucy, suggested a narrow boat and that would make it easier for me to join them most evenings. On board were our three children plus a friend and her baby. It is a really relaxing way to spend a holiday. Everybody loved it."

The actor ***John Nettles***, said he was driving along a quiet road in Cornwall.

"I was aware that my petrol supply was running low, so I stopped and asked an old man where the nearest petrol station was. 'I don't know,' he replied, looking gloomily at the ground. 'But it doesn't matter much. This road ends in half a mile!"

The newspaper columnist, ***Carol Sarlor***, was visiting Sheffield and found herself hopelessly lost. She stopped a man. "He was quite the friendliest soul you ever met North of the M25," said Carol. "I confessed I was a total stranger to the area and asked for directions to the Cathedral. 'Aye,' he muttered, 'It's easy. You go up there, turn right and keep going 'till you get to where there was a pub called the Star. It's not there any more, but you turn left where it used to be and you're almost there."

National holidays ran a trip to see the Blackpool lights. The passengers had been told they had four hours in the resort before returning to the coach. Half-an-hour before departure, three, twenty-something lads, bumped into someone they saw at their local every Saturday night. He was definitely the worse for wear.

"I didn't know you were on this trip." said Keith. Paul was incomprehensible and seemed to mumble something about another coach, so the lads took him back to the bus. When they arrived back in Hull they returned him to his home - only to find that all his family were on a weeks holiday in Blackpool.

I met the late ***Les Dawson*** in Bridlington, after a performance at the Spa Theatre and typical of the man, came down to the bar to chat to all the boys in the band.

We got talking briefly about holidays and relaxation and Les said he loved to motor over to the Lake District.

"Anywhere in particular?" I asked.

"Not really, but I did like the Trough of Bowland. It's so picturesque."

"Don't you go abroad?" I queried.

"I hate going abroad," he told me, "Absolutely hate it. It's awful. I once went to Gibraltar." He raised his eyes heavenwards. "Only because I was working there. They offered me a lot of money so I decided to give it a go. I found the whole sorry episode horrendous. I couldn't wait to get home."

SCOTLAND

While motoring around Scotland for two weeks in May, a Californian couple managed the whole spectrum of British weather. They'd had rain, hail, fog, even floods.

A sympathetic Scot was commiserating with them about their ruined holiday, when one of the Americans stopped him in his tracks. "Oh, for heaven's sake, stop apologising. It's been absolutely wonderful."

The Scot thought he was hearing things. "Wonderful! he exclaimed. "What on earth do you mean?"

"It's wonderful. We've just loved being in Scotland when the weather was happening."

ORKNEYS

Lying twenty miles off the Scottish mainland, Orkney comprises 70 islands, 18 of which are inhabited. Mainland and Hoy being the largest.

Green rolling hills, prehistoric antiquities and rare birds abound.

You take a ferry from Scrabster to Stromness, then you can catch an inter-island ferry service.

When I toured Ireland I couldn't help but notice the lyrical quality of the place names. The Scottish islands seem a bit dour in comparison. For example; Grimness, Gritley, Scrabness and Hackland. Oh, with one exception, well it's not exactly lyrical but I think you'll agree it does have a certain something. Twatt!

I bet playwright ***Alan Plater*** and his vivacious wife Shirley noticed it when they were in the Orkneys for the filming of the series Oliver's Travels, with ***Alan Bates*** and ***Sinead Cusak***, for which Alan had written the script.

Alan told me : "I just love islands. Over the last decade or so we've had a love affair with the Orkneys, starting when I first read George Mackay Brown, the Orcadian poet and story teller. The Orkneys have a history that is five thousand miles deep. They are bleak, tough and beautiful - but not pretty. The economy relies on ferries that link the various islands. Since I was born in Jarrow and many of my forebears worked in ship-building, I'm fascinated by ships. I can watch them like other people watch trains.

Many of my best memories are linked to television projects and this is one."

Alan once sent me a postcard extolling the beauty of the islands. The comment was: "It was beautiful." followed with the rider. "I expect it still is."

WALES

In the eighties, ***George Melley*** bought a medieval tower. He said: "I spend every spare minute I can there. I bomb around the area on a scooter but my main interest is fishing. "I know people think it's the most boring thing on earth but it gets you in touch with nature."

George considers it has everything. "You laze out on a grassy knoll then suddenly a fish bites and the rush of adrenaline spurs you to action and when its all over it's back to the grassy knoll."

GREECE

"Like most actors," said ***Leslie Grantham***, "all my holidays have to be quick breaks to fit in with work. So I often take pot luck. I once jumped on a plane bound for Athens, arriving at four in the morning, we took the first boat leaving for an island and wound up in a fantastic little flat above a great restaurant run by a female Demis Roussos for £4 a night. The snag was the Greek wine. How anyone swallows Retsina, I don't understand. And Demestica is surely much better for cleaning toilets. The island was Paros and I found out they plant the vines all higgly piggly. The idea is that if God wants them to grow, they'll grow."

The debonair ***Francis Matthews*** was on an away from it all holiday in Greece with his family, when he had an urgent call from his agent.

"You've been offered three days work in Norway," he said.
"Great," said Francis, "But why ring me on holiday?"

"Ah, that's the snag," said his agent, "They want you the day after tomorrow."

"No chance," said Mr Mathews, "I'm having a super time. It can't be worth going all that way and missing part of my holiday."

His agent told him: "The Norwegians are prepared to pay you enough to cover the full cost of the holiday."

"So I had no hesitation," said Francis, "I accepted immediately. I went into a local travel agents to make arrangements. I was told that the best, in fact the only way, was to catch a ferry to Athens, this would take about five hours, then catch a flight to Scandinavia.

A very early start was essential. My wife waved me off happily on the first leg of my journey.

I ate a hearty breakfast on board the ferry and was relaxing on deck, casually checking all my documents when horror upon horrors, I realised I'd brought my wife's passport. I was trapped on that bloody ferry for another three and a half hours. I stood up, I sat down, I paced, I strode around, I ranted quietly to myself and checked my watch every ten minutes. The journey was interminable.

I got a taxi to the airport but was advised under no circumstances would I be allowed to travel without my own passport.

I sprinted out of the airport and leapt into the nearest cab and headed for the British Embassy. Guess what? They were closed - all bloody day! I was by now desperate. 'How much to take me back to the villa?' I asked the taxi driver. He quoted me about £190, round trip. 'Let's go' I shouted. Eight hours later, I was back home. It was midnight. Rushing through the villa, I grabbed the passport and rushed out with my wife, barely awake, demanding an explanation. 'I'll ring,' I shouted as I climbed back into the taxi.

At Athens airport a very understanding airline clerk, checked all the available flights and told me the only way she could get me to my destination on time was via, Paris, Frankfurt and Geneva. I didn't have a choice. I went for it.

I arrived almost exactly twenty-four hours late. Without a rehearsal, I was just plunged into the show."

I was impressed and asked him if it had gone okay.

"No problem," said Mr M, in fact it was a resounding success.

The journey home was uneventful, so I was then left to enjoy my holiday in peace."

CRETE

On trip round the island, we visited Knossos, the former home of King Midas.

There we were all admiring the Queen's bathroom with what was supposedly the first WC in history with running water. They went on at such lengths about it, I'm surprised they didn't want us all to give it a try!

After witnessing this marvel of ancient technology I wondered why Crete's modern day sanitation had not markedly improved since 1700BC.

Oh I know one area you'd like, that's the Zeppos restaurant on the waterfront at Hania Harbour. It serves mouth-watering swordfish while you watch the world go by and it boasts flush toilets!

This restaurant is held in high esteem among all the eateries around the harbour and the owner told us proudly that once Sir Geoffrey Howe dropped in for supper, after being recommended by a visiting diplomat - so there!.

Race Davies - actress - says she had a holiday disaster in Crete.

"I was one of those silly tourists who hire motorcycles and wear shorts and no crash helmet. I fell off and was so badly gashed you could see the bone in my knee. A British couple drove me to the nearest village but there was no doctor, so the villagers poured surgical spirit over the wound. When I returned to London my leg had swollen like an elephant's and doctors had to remove bits of glass and grime which were still embedded in it, with running water."

CEPHALONIA

An avalanche of drachmas were raining down on the residents of this Greek island when ***Nicolas Cage*** and ***John Hurt*** filmed Louis de Bernieres' bestseller Captain Corelli's Mandolin. While Nicholas Cage, was holed up in a 15th-century mountainside villa, he complained continually about the heat, while John Hurt and the female lead ***Penelope Cruz*** were spending lavishly in local tavernas and flea markets.

But one of the biggest recipients of the film company's cash was a mournful farmer in this remote island. He rented out his donkey at a daily rate of £80 a day, for the production. He was asked why the sad face.

"Because I'm only getting £20 a day to look after the animal."

Like they say there's no pleasing some people

ITHACA

Legendary resting place of Homer's Odysseus. To get there you have to take a bus from Cephalonia airport to the ferry. Let me warn you it can be a pretty rough crossing and on my trip more than a few passengers - including me - were in dire need of a medicinal brandy, or two. A taxi takes everyone to their accommodation.

This is the real Greece with scented paths, whitewashed walls, sienna roofs and arched belfries reaching up to cloudless skies. Kioni only has two tavernas. One classy the other for locals.

Take the walk to the inland village of Stavros, one of the suggested sites of Odysseus's palace.

It's idyllic, not a whiff of traffic or noise, completely untouched by mass tourism - they only have one bus. You'll find hidden coves and the ruins of a small hotel once frequented by ***Winston Churchill.***

Another must. The tiny village of Anogi. During the 1953 earthquake, a tremor shook the plaster off the walls to reveal immaculate frescoes, painted 800 years ago by grateful Cretan monk's, who fled from the Turks and founded a refuge in Ithaca.

Go on try that ferry trip from Cephalonia - You know it makes sense.

MYKONOS

This is the island beloved of transvestites and the beautiful people.

In the picturesque harbour, you are entertained by the two fattest pelicans I have ever seen.

Cobbled, winding streets lead you into a maze of small, white-washed shops, selling designer labels at exorbitant prices.

Evenings can be spent outdoors relaxing in an open-air fish restaurant, as the fingers of golden sunsets reach out and entwine you in their magical glow.

Many of the seafront bars are famous for their transvestite entertainment and the talent is extraordinary. I only visited one, not because I objected but because they were all prettier than me!

This was a favourite holiday destination of the late ***Kenneth Williams***. He told me he would check into a naturist resort, miles way from the hurly burly of the harbour.

"It was marvellous." he enthused. "The food was wonderful, the sun was always shining and everyone else was nude, so you could let it all hang out. The freedom was wonderful."

RHODES

I remember taking a trip around the island and we stopped for a refreshing drink. The name of the taverna? Sunburnt Arms.

Well it amused me.

HIMALAYAS

A vast mountain system in central Asia and I'm sure you know, it is the highest mountain range in the world.

Sarah Kennedy said she was trekking through the mountains when they stopped at a monastery and was asked if she'd like to partake of tea made with yak's milk. "Then would you believe, a monk asked if I'd like to visit his cell. Well you must admit it's one up on etchings! Anyway it was completely bare except for his bed and a Pirelli calendar on the wall. Bare boobs and bottoms abounding." She giggled. "Talk about your cup runneth over!"

HONG KONG

D*avid Janson* couldn't wait to tell me all about his wedding to actress ***Debbie Arnold***.

"We both wanted a quiet wedding, without the usual showbiz razzmatazz. But I had to leave Debbie as I was setting off for Hong Kong in a ***Derek Nimmo*** production and I knew the city would be perfect for our wedding. Faxes winged their way to and fro but with only two days before the tour began, the answer came back. 'Sorry but you have to be resident in Hong Kong fourteen days and the tour was only for eleven.

Debbie was so disappointed but she said to compensate she would fly out to see me for the final few days of the tour."

"When she arrived, a reception was being held for the cast, with some very important dignitaries present. We were telling one, who was wearing more gold braid than Prince Philip, of our disappointment at not being able to tie the knot in that special city. 'Don't worry,' he told us, 'I'll fix everything for you. Just be at the registry office about mid-day tomorrow. Everything will be okay."

You can guess we were over the moon. We could hardly sleep and first thing next morning, we rushed out and purchased some suitable wedding apparel.

Come twelve -o-clock and we were waiting on the steps. True to his word, our knight in golden braid had managed to cut through all the red tape and we could get married." He smiled at the memory and continued. "When we returned to the hotel a reception had been arranged. There was a magnificent ice-carving across the doorway. The cast presented us with a set of luggage and some carved figures to remind us of that special day. As if we'd ever forget it. It was so romantic. And you'll never guess what the hotel had done as a special treat?"

I shook my head.

"They'd only allocated the bridal suite for us. A perfect ending to a perfect day."

Eating can sometimes be a bit problematical in far flung destinations. The Far East in particular. The natives idea of a good nosh is not exactly our idea of a gourmet meal. I do try most things, including fried brick which I sampled in Tunisia - this was a delicious crispy pancake, with a softly boiled egg inside, served like a fan, on a cut out orange - but I stopped at the suggestion I should try, animal penises, although the guide tried to convince me they were delicious. I, like ***Paul O'Grady*** - aka Lily Savage - managed to avoid temptation.

Michael Palin renowned for his globe trotting antics, confessed ; "In my travels I have been obliged to eat some rather adventurous local delicacies." He went on to say that at one feast he was served with the local gastronomic delight...bull's testicles!

"They were slightly cold and a bit unpleasant," confessed Mr Palin. "They were a bit like black pudding with stringy lumps, though they weren't as disgusting as I thought they might be. They were sliced, so they didn't look as if they were genitalia."

Oh, that's all right then Michael!

I was in a restaurant in Bangkok and as my first course was placed before me, I saw a maggot happily doing the breast stroke. I called the waiter over and he immediately took the offending bowl away. He returned beaming. “There you are English lady,” he said and placed the bowl back on the table. “I take out wiggly thing for you.”

INDIA

M*ary Nightingale*, travel presenter, admitted; "It's not all glamour you know. When I went to Goa in India for an episode of Wish You Were here...? we were unable to get a domestic flight across the country, so the camera crew and I decided to go by train, which should have taken eight hours but ended up taking nineteen. To make matters worse, there was a rat running up and down the corridor!"

Actor ***Richard Briars*** took every precaution when he headed out on a pilgrimage to India, where his mother was born.

"I'd never been anywhere that different before and I have to admit I'm very nervous." Then mischievously added. "But I gather it's a good place to lose weight."

Richard's mother was born near Calcutta, the daughter of a British consul, in the last days of the Raj. Now, armed only with a bag of old photographs, he wanted to find out about her childhood.

He mused: "I'm bound to get ill and I'll be taking water purifying tablets and anything else I can get my hands on."

Fear of flying usually keeps Richard at home when it comes to holidays.

"I'll have to swig a very large vodka to get me in the air." he said.

IRELAND

Hull born ***John Alderton*** and his wife ***Pauline Collins*** loved visiting County Kerry. They stayed in a chalet in the mountains near a small village, set beside a tranquil lake.

DUBLIN

The city has everything and within minutes you can be in glorious countryside.

There are over 1,000 pubs in Dublin and at every street corner I saw musicians.

I had been told a visit to O'Neills bar was a must, so decided to try it - just to sample the atmosphere you understand. Outside, three children sang their hearts out in raucous voices and played jigs on their tin whistles.

I staggered out at 1.00am, having fallen victim, not to the local Guinness, but to conversations with a dozen or so wonderful characters. We exchanged worldly thoughts, which included whether ***Michael Shumaker*** was a better driver than ***Stirling Moss***, is a man wearing nothing but a pair of grey wool socks a turn off, and how do snails make love?

At my hotel in Dublin, I asked the night porter, "Tomorrow, could I have a wake-up call at 8.15 please and a copy of the Daily Express. He nodded and turned to write down my requests.

The following morning I was woken at six am. "Hello, it's your night porter here. Your newspapers have arrived. Would you like me to bring it up now or would you rather wait 'till the wake-up call?"

Judy Cornwell - who can forget her memorable performance as Hyacinth Bucket's, sister-in-law in 'Keeping up Appearances' - had to go to Dublin to do some research on a book she was writing. "I didn't tell a soul I was going," said Judy, "and I finished my research quicker than anticipated. I was having a wonderful time. Completely independent and not beholden to anyone, so I thought before I go back I'll go and have a look at the isle of Aran. So this newly liberated lady hired a car and set off. The island is about thirty miles from the mainland across Galway Bay.

"When I arrived I immediately booked in a small hotel then leaving my small suitcase behind I set off exploring with a bottle of Perrier Water and a bar of chocolate for sustenance.

I just kept beetling along admiring the rolling countryside and absolutely revelling in my new found freedom and kept on motoring. I suddenly realised all the road signs were in Gaelic, so decided I'd had enough of freedom and turned to return to the hotel - or so I thought - No matter which way I turned I seemed to arrive back at the same cross-roads. I must have tried four times. The cows in a nearby field were highly amused. They'd never seen such activity. A little red car trolling by every ten minutes.

It was getting darker by the minute. Maybe, I thought, there wasn't quite so much to being a modern woman after all. There was no sign of any human beings, just this herd, which seemed to grow by the minute, of inquisitive cattle and sheep.

I got out of my little motor and checked a nearby signpost. I was concentrating on reading it, when a flock of starlings swooped out from the hedgerow and frenetically swirled and circled around my bonnet." (By the way we're talking the cars, not Judy's here.) "They looked like oily rags in a storm. I was terrified and seriously thought about the foolishness of attempting this trip. A lot of swearing and more prayers and I thought I'd have one more go. As I switched on the engine I watched with horror, as the petrol gauge swung ominously to the red, empty sign.

I dumbly wondered if the hotel would send out a search party. But it was a god forsaken place and by now pitch black. Even the bloody cows had now lost interest.

I made the momentous decision, if I didn't come across any sign of human habitation in the next ten minutes - and if the petrol didn't dry up - I'd have to settle down for the night in the car.

I was starving and berated myself for indulging an hour or so earlier. I could hardly see where I was going through the tears which were by now flooding down my face. I was down to a thumb sucking, teddy cuddling three year-old.

The independent lady had vanished forever. My eyes were red and swollen, but suddenly I noticed something shining in the distance. It had to be lights. I jammed my foot hard on the accelerator and sped towards civilisation. But after about ten yards I came to a spluttering halt. The petrol had gone. I got out, yes they were lights. I ran, this time the tears were of joy. It was my hotel.

Evidently I'd only been a matter of yards away all the time, but it was out of my sight.

It was such a relief, but I tell you what," she confided, "If I venture out on my own again, if there ever is a next time, I'll take four chocolate bars!"

When I went on a motoring holiday, taking in the area around Tipperary. I was impressed by some of the place names. We went through Borris. Fifty or sixty miles on we were in Borris-in-Ossory. Names prefixed with Bally, abound. Ballyduff,

Ballydesmond, Ballydehob and Ballycotton and I found my two favourites while heading for Limerick. Ballybunion and Ballispittle!

Also various Heads, litter the landscape. Hags Head, Loop Head, Cods Head, Sheeps Head and Old Head. Oh and what about Skibbereen? Wonderful.

At one point, we got lost, so we went into a small village pub. and asked the barman what was the quickest way to Waterford. "Are you walking or driving?" he asked.

"We're in the car," we told him.

"You're okay then," he replied. "That's the quickest."

After visiting Waterford, we headed for the Boggeragh Mountains and had just checked into a rather remote, white-washed cottage. The small, silver-haired lady, dressed in black from head to toe welcomed us enthusiastically. She handed over the key and pointed up the stairs with a cheery remark: "You hurry up now, do you hear. I'll sure be having a warming pot o' tea for you in twenty minutes."

Ah, how nice, we thought. As we reached the top of the stairs we noticed a sign on room 8, which read.'Notice. In case of fire, the ladder is in room 12.'

We were in room 12. This in itself was confusing as there could only have been three or four bedrooms in the place. We entered and put our case on the bed. Where the hell was that all important ladder? People could be relying on us to save their lives. Then I spied something lurking on the top of the wardrobe. We checked. Bingo! it was the ladder - a rope one - We checked the window. It had obviously not been opened since Gladstone was a boy. Twenty minutes later found us trotting down the stairs for our "warming cup of tea." It was coffee.

ISRAEL

Generation Game girl, ***Francine Lewis*** was asked what her first holiday memory was and she said it had to be when she was seven. "We had a family holiday in Israel. It was the first time I had flown, so I was very excited. Unfortunately, on my first day playing in the sea, a freak wave pulled me under and I almost drowned. As a result I now never swim in the sea."

This didn't stop her falling in love with the country. She says, "Eilat is my favourite holiday destination. I consider myself in heaven when I can enjoy long dinners in the evening under the stars."

Maeve Binchy, said one summer when she was about 22, or 23, she spent the summer in a Kibbutz, plucking chickens and picking oranges. She wrote about the life to her parents and "My father thought it was such an entertaining story he had it typed, sent it to a newspaper and it was published. From that point I started writing travel articles."

ITALY

ROME

The late ***Roy Castle*** swore this was a true story. A Portuguese passenger arrived at Rome airport and was seen standing around rather forlornly. An Air Italia stewardess went up to him and asked if she could help. His English was very limited and his Italian non-existent, so she shepherded him to the help desk. His passport told them his nationality, so arranged for an interpreter. He told the young woman he thought there would be a message from his brother. “He said he would meet me at the airport.”

Although they made numerous calls on the tannoy, in Italian, English and Portuguese, no-one came forward. They quizzed the passenger some more. It turned out he thought he was in New York. He was completely unperturbed as his brother had mentioned there were a lot of Italians in New York

Sarah Kennedy, who hosts the Radio 2 early morning show had booked, what she thought would be a peaceful week away in a villa not far from Rome, with her boy-friend.

Suffice to say, the week-end she decided to fly there was a horrendous computer crash at the air traffic control centre. She started with a seven hour delay. This should have forewarned her.

“I should have arrived at the accommodation about lunchtime but it was past ten p.m. and dark. As I stumbled up the path I noticed leant against the wall, on the terrace a huge tennis racquet.

"Oh is there a tennis court?" I asked hopefully.

"No," replied the guide, "that's for swatting hornets."

"I thought it could only get better," said Sara hopefully, "But I was wrong, it never stopped raining the whole week and we had a further, four delay at Rome airport, on our return."

PISA

When they were visiting Italy, ***Matthew Kelly*** and his family decided to go to Pisa and see the famous leaning tower.

"My wife suffers from vertigo," he told me, "so would only walk half-way up. Stay there I told her, I'll go to the top with the children and collect you on the way down. She wasn't very happy but eventually agreed.

When we arrived at the top there was only a small guard rail which seemed to be at an angle of 45 degrees. I felt absolutely panic stricken. My mouth was opening and shutting like a dying Guppy and not a word came out. The children were completely unaware of the potential danger and I had to grip their tiny hands in a vice like grip, but that of course left me nothing to hang onto. Honestly, I was in a state of complete terror." and as Matthew so succinctly put it, "My trousers were immediately transformed into the brown patchy type. When I managed to get back to the level I'd left the wife, I thought she could take care of the children while I cleaned myself up. Not a chance. By the time we arrived she was a quivering wreck and almost hysterical, so I had to take charge and usher everyone down to the base of the tower. I thought maybe if I didn't sit down, I wouldn't be too uncomfortable!"

I bet anyone who anyone who walked his way that day, would wonder at the aroma wafting in the Italian sunshine. Definitely not your average aftershave pong.

VENICE

Alan Plater and his wife Shirley love to spend Christmas with their family, but one year they told me that with the permission from their children and grandchildren, they spent Christmas in Venice.

"It was bitterly cold," said Alan, "and at a concert in the Vivaldi Church we could not only hear but see the music coming from the singers mouths. On Christmas Eve we ate in a restaurant overlooking St. Marks Square and watched the flood waters rising. When it was time to go, all the customers were supplied with thigh boots and we paddled through the kitchens, out by the back door and were guided to dry land were we handed in our boots."

Another story from ***Sarah Kennedy***, she said: "I paid what I thought was an exorbitant price for a ride on a gondola. Back in the hotel I mentioned this to a fellow traveller and she told me I was lucky. She'd evidently climbed aboard the craft for a lovely romantic ride, when the boatman held out his hands to help her aboard with the words. 'Hop aboard love.' What a shock', said the lady and she couldn't help commenting on his accent. 'No, you're right love, I'm not Italian, but my step-father is and I've just bought the boat from him.' I asked her what she thought about that," said Sarah. "The lady said her illusions were completely shattered and it wasn't the same somehow."

The actress ***Race Davies*** says she always thinks of Venice as a fairy-tale land.

"The first time I went was with a friend and I just couldn't believe the sights, the art, the food and the gorgeous men. We stayed just outside the city in the Dolomites, surrounded by vineyards and I thought I'd died and gone to Heaven."

Don't try it at Christmas Race.

JAPAN

Many people extol the virtues of the Bullet Train (Tokyo) They are impressed by its cleanliness, but there's a snag. If you want to visit the toilet, beware. You will find yourself squatting over a hole, while clinging to a small hand rail, speeding along at more than 100 miles an hour.

It's amazing with such great technology they haven't yet mastered the art of building a lavatory bowl.

I thought you might like to hear about Mrs Downs, who'd booked a fifteen day trip to Japan. She came into the shop and asked: "Dorothea, I wonder if you could help us. Can you tell me if the people in Japan speak Japanese or English?"

Wow was she in for a culture shock.

We all know how meticulous they are as a nation but a friend of mine found out the hard way when he was visiting Tokyo, early in 2000.

"Suddenly," said Ralph, "Tanks started rumbling through a luxury shopping district we were visiting and we could see soldiers scaling all the big stores in sight. When we looked up, there were helicopters hovering above every skyscraper.

It was terrifying, as we didn't have a clue what was going on. But it turned out it was nothing more alarming than an operation to simulate the military response to an earthquake striking the city. You should have seen the small kids, they were all issued with flame-proof hoods and they had to wear them. That night on the television it said that over 7,00 troops had been involved."

I read in our trade paper that a member of ABTA (The Association of British Travel Agents) had been giving a talk to similar minded folk in Japan. He thought he'd finish one speech with a joke, as he knew quite a few spoke English but his words were still being translated.

"The crowd seemed very amused," he said. "I was feeling very pleased with myself, but felt I should compliment the interpreter as she'd translated my joke very quickly."

"Oh, that's all right," she said, rather non-chalantly, "I just told the audience that the speaker had told a joke and they should now laugh and clap."

Peter Ustinov, the consummate word master, also found out about their attention to detail when he was invited to talk about world refugees.

He'd arrived in Tokyo, where his hosts had arranged an overnight stay before his onward flight to Osaka, the following day, where he was to deliver his speech.

He was comfortably settled in his room when there was a knock at the door. His wife answered only to be met by a small, beaming Japanese gentleman.

"I see Mr Ustinov please?"

He was invited in.

"You Mr Ustinov?" he asked.

Peter said he nodded the affirmative.

"Please I tell you," said the small Japanese person. "We leave hotel at nine am. You please be ready."

Before Mr Ustinov could reply, the gentleman continued. "You be in foyer at eight-fifty-two. That mean you at top of elevator at eight-forty-four. We will give you call at eight-thirty-nine, telling you, you have five minutes only."

By now his wife was almost screaming. "But," said Mr

Ustinov, “they carried out the instructions to the letter.”

“I daren’t do otherwise,” he said to the interviewer, in almost reverential terms.

Upon arrival in Osaka he was told they had set aside forty-five minutes for his speech.

“Forty-five minutes” exploded Mr Ustinov. “I can’t speak for forty-five minutes on refugees.”

He was told he must, to guarantee the smooth running of the evening.

He desperately tried to pad out his twenty minute speech, but after twenty-six, he gave up and sat down.

His hosts were ecstatic.

Peter and his wife were completely mystified.

“You very clever man Mr Ustinov. Very, very clever indeed.”

“I am?” queried Mr Ustinov.

“Oh yes indeed, very clever man. How you know we running nineteen minutes late?”

KENYA

Two special requests I've had from clients booking a safari holiday.

One: "Could you arrange for us to have ground floor rooms please."

They were staying at Treetops!

Then another couple, posed the question.

"We don't have to shoot the animals for food do we?"

But one of my favourites happened while a lady was in the shop asking for details of Kenya. Several brochures were looked at, prices checked and any information I thought relevant, passed on. The client appeared hooked. "I'll have a word with my husband and come back tomorrow."

Good as her word, 9.30am prompt she returned to the office and booked the Cheetah Safari with Kuoni Holidays. As I was finalising the reservation the lady asked: "Can you advise me what sort of clothes I should take with me?"

I was explaining about cotton trousers and long sleeved shirts, when the client suddenly cut me short.

"No, no" she said. "I mean will I be all right in those game reserves if I wear tights, or do you think I should wear a suspender belt?"

Jeremy Spake, the TV presenter, can speak fluent Russian because of his time with Aeroflot, the Russian airline, I also believe his mother was Russian. Anyway he says his favourite destination is Kenya and in particular visiting the Masai Mara.

"I've been so many times now," he said, "that I've got some really great friends there. Kenya offers such a different life to the one we live in Europe. It's a very humbling experience to go there and I just love it."

Matthew Kelly had been invited to climb in Kenya with some English and Kenyan children for a television documentary.

They set off in good spirits, but when they reached about ten thousand feet, three of the British children were overcome with altitude sickness, so a guide returned with them to base camp.

But let Matthew tell the story:

"Another two thousand feet higher and another of the children became ill and had to be taken lower. There was a cabin of sorts at fourteen thousand feet where we had intended to spend the night, before trying to trek to the top which was seventeen thousand feet. But altitude sickness struck all the remaining British children. The Kenyans were fine as they lived at seven thousand feet, so naturally felt no ill effects. A guide took the remaining British children, which only left one guide, me, a doctor, a cameraman and six Kenyan children.

At two am the doctor became violently ill and it was imperative he was taken to sea level as soon as possible.

When dawn broke I was also feeling the effects. It was just as if you had a monumental hangover. We had a big problem as now we had no guides or doctor, and it would have been madness to continue the climb.

"But, " he continued, "It had been an exhilarating experience, albeit marred by mishaps and illness. And I tell you what, " said Matthew, "I've promised myself, one day, I'll return and conquer that seventeen thousand feet."

Actress ***Leila Birch***, who played that man eating waitress Teresa, met her fiancee Paul Harris when they starred alongside each other in a Channel 4 comedy, The Renford Rejects, just before Leila joined the cast of Eastenders.

The couple became engaged on Millennium night on a breach in Kenya. Leila recalls: "Midnight struck and fireworks were going off everywhere. There was a huge party at the hotel but the two of us were on the beach alone. We were dancing around a palm tree singing Auld lang Syne when Paul suddenly dropped to his knees and proposed.

I laughed and walked away thinking he was joking. But when I turned round again he was still there so I realised he meant it."

Leila accepted and as Paul hadn't been able to find a suitable ring, he took a piece of tinsel off a miniature Christmas tree he'd given to her and wrapped it around her finger.

"We'd brought a cassette player onto the beach and a bottle of champagne and we just sat there, all alone on the sand, drinking and listening to the waves. Then we lay down and fell asleep in each others arms. It was such a romantic way to start the new Millennium."

Just a warning if you visit Kenya. I know of a British tourist who while slightly inebriated, tore up the equivalent of £6 worth of Kenyan banknotes. He was told: "Tourist have to respect this country," then they promptly jailed him for three months.

MIDDLE EAST

D*avid Janson* was in Muscat in the Alan Aykbourn play Taking Steps - By the way if you haven't seen it and it comes to a theatre near you, try to see it, it's very funny and original - Anyway, there was David mooching around the hotel shops when an Arab in full flowing robes bore down on him.

He towered above David and poking him in the chest, boomed. "I know you."

"No I don't think so," said David.

"Oh, yes I do." insisted the Arab. "You Kevin."

David protested. "No, you've mistaken me for someone else. My name's David."

But the Arab was not deterred. "No, no, I DO know you. You definitely Kevin."

David said, "No, you've definitely made a mistake. My name is David, not Kevin."

The man in the robes beamed and pronounced. "No, you definitely Kevin. I learn English from you."

Then the penny dropped. About three years earlier, David and his actress wife ***Debbie Arnold*** had done a training video for the Oxford Press.... and his character was called Kevin!

David told me that while they were out there a few of the cast decided to hire a car and slope off to the desert.

"We parked at the side of the road and decided to explore the sand dunes."

"You've never seen anything like it," he said. "The peaks were deep red and we all leapt about bare footed in complete abandonment. We felt as if we were flying, an experience I've never encountered before or since. Suddenly we realised we couldn't see the car or the road! We had all been whooping with joy but I can tell you it soon came to an abrupt end. 'Don't panic, now we haven't got to panic,' said one enterprising member of the cast. Who was he kidding?" asked David "It was easier said than done. But it all ended well. We sensibly decided to follow the sun as we were sure it was behind us when we started out and we were sure we hadn't walked that far. You wouldn't believe the stillness as we plodded up and down those huge dunes of shifting sand. Our eyes were everywhere trying to catch sight of the road. Then somebody spotted a silver ribbon in the distance and sitting in isolation was our red Mercedes We were home, well nearly, but wow, did it serve as a salutary lesson."

MORROCCO

TV presenter *Carolyn Marshall* said, "I can't go anywhere without some sort of accident or health problem cropping up while I'm away."

In fact it happened so often, she just couldn't decide where to spend her honeymoon in case something happened to spoil it. She admitted. "I would have loved to go to the Galapagos islands off South America, and get into all that Darwinian stuff but me and the sun simply don't mix.

"We had also thought about a rambling holiday in the Scottish Highlands, then realised that was a no-no. Midges absolutely love me and bite me to bits," said Carolyn.

"In fact the last time I went anywhere really hot was Morocco a few years back, but I spent the whole time languishing on the beach covered in a white sheet. It's not just the sun, I'm the insects, I'm their favourite person. I have to admit I'm also horribly accident prone."

"I have the most dreadful accidents whenever I go on holiday," she says. "When ever I go away my mother answers the phone and says, "Oh no. What's happened this time?"

"Once it was a fractured scull when I walked into a glass door - I've still got the bump on my forehead today. Another time I fell fully clothed into a swimming pool and nearly drowned.

"Oh and one time I was knocked off my bike and left unconscious."

Now that's what I call being accident prone.

Here's a story I thought you might like.

A Moroccan man was found dead in his bed. The coroner said, "There were no marks on his body, but the autopsy revealed he had large amounts of methane gas in his system. Relatives have confirmed to me that his diet consisted of cabbage and beans, exactly the right combination of foods to produce large quantities of methane."

It appears that he had been repeatedly passing wind and died by gassing himself in his very small airtight room.

Claire Raynor said she was sitting astride a very sullen camel when a woman rushed up to her and said, "Oh, Claire, how lovely to see you. I have this terrible problem...!"

PORTUGAL

Sir *Cliff Richard* has a restored farmhouse in the Algarve. It's a six-bedroomed property near Faro and boasts its own vineyard.

I met ***Bruce Forsyth*** while he was performing in a country club in Yorkshire.

My husband was the compere and on the first night I was invited back stage to say hello.

A couple of nights later he invited Ray and I to have supper with him and his M.D ***Don Black***.

He was great company and we discussed many things, including a story about a friend of his who had hired a villa for a family holiday on the Algarve.

The son's girl friend got extremely sun burnt. It was quite late in the evening before she realised how bad it was. None of them had thought to take any cream or lotions, so one suggestion seemed quite sensible. Sprinkle talcum powder on the burnt areas.

She returned from the bathroom complaining the talcum was like sand and it was now hurting more than ever.

It was the following morning before they realised that she'd used a tin which was beside the sink. They checked it in the phrase book and found she been using Portuguese scouring powder!

Ouch!!

Judith Chalmers, the well-known travel presenter was so enamoured with Vale de Lobo in the Algarve, the family bought a house there.

"We bought it in 1973," said Judith, "and we still adore it."

"It's such a wonderful place for all the family, full of great little fish cafes, lively town markets and some fabulous beaches. The men play golf while I enjoy exploring the mountains, buying terracotta pots along the way."

Another personality who has property in the Algarve is the actor ***Michael Elphick***. It's situated in a small fishing village where he can relax and completely escape from the pressures of his craft. He is reported to do a great deal of swimming. In fact he calls it his 'haven in the sun.'

ROMANIA

Just a quickie from ***Alan Plater*** who said: "Without doubt the scariest time I ever encountered was in Ceausescu's Romania where we had close encounters with currency smugglers, bugged telephones and frightened people. Quite the saddest place I've ever visited."

RUSSIA

Do you know who the first cowboys were? Well according to an American archaeologist, they lived on the Russian Steppes, just North of the Red Sea.

They were the first people who thought of actually riding horses, instead of eating them. They estimate it was about 5,500 years ago. They called these primitive cowboys, the Sredni Stig.

'Ride 'em Sredni Stog' doesn't have the same ring somehow!

When ***Mark Curry***, was travelling to Russia with ***Yvette Fielding*** and ***Caron Keating***, on a Blue Peter assignment, they found that in every hotel they checked into, only four rooms had been allocated for a party of eighteen. Fifteen crew and three presenters.

Mark told me: "We checked into the first hotel and we were told we had to share. Fine we said, but then found we were expected to share up to five in a room."

"We were not amused and decided, if it happened again, we would try the Russian way of complaining, because if we spoke English, it was always, 'sorry, no speak.'

We'd finished filming and travelled to the next location. We were taken to the hotel and found once again only four rooms had been reserved, so we all stood in the foyer, with suitcases and equipment scattered around us. Everytime, someone approached us, we very firmly said 'niet.'

We had to repeat it again and again and again, as the Russians had done to us on previous occasions. Our resolve never wavered." said Mark, then confessed, "Oh, well maybe just a little bit, but we certainly weren't going to admit it.

We were determined, but we did get a bit worried when bodies, started rushing about and shouting at us in Russian. It was quite alarming. But we stood our ground.

After about an hour, miraculously, another four rooms were spirited out of the air for us. We'd won."

Mark gave that mischievous grin of his and added, "We were all muttering 'niet' in our sleep for days afterwards."

Claire Raynor said she was on a visit to Moscow when a lady approached and asked her to adopt her nephew, so he could get a British citizenship.

"My husband, Des. suggested, tongue in cheek, we could find him a nice English bride as well. She beamed at Des. and said, 'Good idea. You fix!"

Several years ago, Singer ***Suzi Quatro*** had been booked on a tour of Russia and decided to take her children with her.

"We had what I call a working holiday. It was two months long and I can honestly say it was fantastic. The children got to see places they would never see ordinarily, like Leningrad, Moscow, Odessa, Lithuania and Georgia. We never usually have time for holidays, because I'm always working. But I try to take the children with us wherever we go, trying to arrange around school as much as possible."

I don't know where to start with my recollections of Russia. Some, in fact most, are quite extraordinary, so I think I'll leave most of those memories for another book.

But I can't resist telling you about the sign I saw at the zoo:

"PLEASE DO NOT FEED THE ANIMALS. IF YOU HAVE ANY SUITABLE FOOD, PLEASE GIVE IT TO THE GUARDS."

Or the guide who was asked to convert 'Out of sight out of mind' for her Russian companions. Another Russian in the party disagreed with her. He told us that she'd given the literal translation which was: "Invisible idiot."

Well she wasn't wrong was she?

Makes you wonder about all those important summits with world leaders relying completely on one persons translation.

And I can't go without telling you about our 'special gourmet meal. We were told "It is a night you will not forget." I couldn't argue with that.

On the menu; Squirrel soup and boiled cabbage - the cabbage came in a wine glass, well it was supposed to be posh, and no I didn't try the soup, but without doubt they were responsible for serving me the worst apple pie I have ever tasted in my life. The pips hadn't been taken out and they still had the stalks attached. But worst of all it was flavoured with salt!

Oh, by the way, did you know that one in three people in the world are communists?

Just thought I'd toss that in.

SEYCHELLES

D*erek Jameson* said he went to the Seychelles and was looking forward to it immensely. "I thought I was going to paradise he said, "but it was appalling."

"You wouldn't believe the problems we had. Delays were everywhere and to cap it all we'd chosen the rainy season. I couldn't wait to get home.

I know how he felt because the first time I went it was also the rainy season. When we checked in, reception presented us with our room keys and a golf umbrella!

The accommodation was in thatched chalets around the grounds. But it didn't deter us, we had a wonderful time - It was a bit like a cup of tea really. Wet and warm.

I loved the island and the people and someone who agrees with me wholeheartedly is the gorgeous *Tracy Shaw*, who plays the hairdresser Maxine in Coronation Street.

She will tell anyone who cares to listen about the outstanding beauty of the island. She flew to the Indian Ocean paradise for a holiday with her mum, Ann, staying on the island of La Digue, at the luxury hotel, The Plantation Club.

Tracy said: "We wandered through dunes as soft as silk and were taken to a wonderful exotic jungle. Although it was very hot we both cooled off by snorkelling and scuba diving."

SINGAPORE

Singapore was always a popular stop-over for my clients on their way to Australia. One very satisfied customer had stayed in the New Otani Hotel and at his request they had forwarded me a price list with the following letter;

"Dear Ms Desforges,

We are referred to you by Mr and Mrs Bent Bods and are pleased to offer rates.

Sincerely, The manager.

Nothing wrong with that you say - except the name of my client was a Mr and Mrs Bert Boots.

John Prescott, MP was returning from Singapore, where he'd purchased a video camera. He quite properly gone through the red channel, knowing he would have duty to pay, but the receipts he presented to the custom's officer, did not tally with what they thought it should have cost. Mr Prescott was adamant they were correct but ended up having to pay the extra duty required. He immediately put in an appeal.

I never did find out if he won.

SOUTH AFRICA

P*aul O'Grady* (Lily Savage) said he visited South Africa in'99.

"The place where I stayed rang a bell like a fire alarm when animals appeared outside. But I didn't know that. So we were all in this place and the bell rang and I thought, 'oh my god, a fire!' and ran outside where we found that we were surrounded by lions. Let me tell you I ran pretty quickly back inside."

SPAIN

A drunken break in Ibiza with pals at the age of seventeen put Streetmate presenter ***Davina McCall*** off alcohol for life.

"I went with three mates for a four night break. As you can imagine it was a clubbers mayhem. The day we arrived I did something I'd never, ever done before - I got blind drunk."

"Nobody warned us about Spanish measures. There was practically half-a-bottle in just one tequila slammer! So never, ever again."

Another boozy holiday was sampled by Coronation Street actor, ***Simon Wright.***

Well not so much him, as his friends.

"I went to Magaluf with two mates." he said: "We partied all night - or until my friends had drunk too much. I don't drink, so I kept dancing until the early morning. Then I'd get up and after just a couple of hours in bed and kip throughout the day on the beach. It was heaven. In fact, up to now, that's the only holiday where I've had a problem.

We were waiting at the carousel for our cases and they never arrived. Then the coach left without us and we were left at the airport while they searched for our bags. They eventually found them four hours later, so it was nearly 5am before we reached our hotel. We were absolutely exhausted the next day but we soon got over it!"

Don't book a holiday with a friend you barely know. A guaranteed recipe for disaster.

Francine Lewis can vouch for that. She said it happened to her when she booked a last minute trip with a girl who was more an acquaintance than a friend.

"The only thing we had in common was that we had just broken up with our boyfriends. I let her organise the whole thing, and we ended up in a cheap hotel in Lanzarote which stank of sewerage and had insects in the bed!"

Putting all your spare money, passports etc. in the hotel's safety deposit boxes is always a good idea, but it's amazing the lengths people will go to secreting their valuables, rather than pay the very modest fee asked for by hotels and in many cases you'll find it's a completely free service.

The lovely ***Tom O'Connor*** said a friend of his decided to hide his house keys, passport and English money in a hole he found in the wall behind the wash basin.

"All went well for a couple of days," said Tom, "but he returned one afternoon after visit to Palma and found the hole had been well and truly plastered over.

It cost him the equivalent of £15 to recover his possessions and have the hole re-plastered."

GRAN CANARIA

I was on an educational to the Canary Islands and made friends with a member of staff from Briggs and Hill in Halifax. He told me their agency is right next door to the Civic Theatre's stage door, and when the annual pantomime comes to town, they never know who might pop in.

"Last year, ***Danny La Rue*** came in for some brochures and the year before that it was ***Ken Dodd***. But our Kirstin was swooning over some actor from Neighbours. He didn't want to book anything - he was just looking for the nearest gymnasium."

IBIZA

Former Eastenders star ***Des Coleman*** (he played the loveable Lenny) was on the island shooting a film based on the night-club scene and on a day off, went jet-skiing.

He lost control in the waters near Cala Tarida beach south of San Antonio. He immediately got into difficulties, as he is a very poor swimmer.

Lifeguards had to give him the kiss of life during the twenty minutes it took an ambulance to arrive. He was rescucitated on the beach but rushed to hospital unconscious. He was put on a 24-hour ventilator to help him breathe, but after a few days rest he made a good recovery.

MARBELLA

Sean Connery used to be seen regularly among the jet-setters in Marbella, but got fed up with the constant attention from holidaymakers and sold his villa. He used to enjoy taking his speedboat out but always tried to go to some secluded area where he wouldn't be pestered by tourists.

I met ***Michael Medwin***, the actor, when he was appearing in a play in Hull. He told me: "I'd been working hard so my wife and I decided to jet off for a week to a very exclusive hotel in Southern Spain."

"You know the sort," he said, "It's expected that all men should wear dinner suits, so we carefully packed our best clobber and headed off for a well earned rest. We arrived at about lunch time and after unpacking we decided to take a leisurely stroll around the grounds. We returned about tea-time and started to prepare for dinner. We'd both showered and were dressed in our finery when the dreadful truth dawned. I'd forgotten to pack any shoes. It was too late to go out and purchase some, so I had to go to dinner wearing a black, double breasted evening suit, bow-tie and hush puppies."

He looked heavenwards and groaned. "Very tatty hush-puppies. I was mortified. I walked closely behind my wife, hoping her long, glamorous evening dress would help conceal my unusual footwear. I wasn't too bothered, as I thought it would only be for one night and I could pop out the next day and buy a pair. Wrong! It was only a flaming bank holiday and everything was shut. I wouldn't mind," confessed Michael, "but I honestly don't think a single person noticed, or I suppose cared, what I had on my feet."

It was also in Marbella that ***Jilly Johnson*** says she had a holiday disaster.

She confessed, "Actually it was all my own fault. I took all my money and passport to the beach. Then I decided I would have a quick dip. I thought I had a good view of the bag but in an instant it was gone. I was not insured and ended up spending the rest of my holiday in the British Consulate and had to borrow money from friends. Now I never go anywhere without full insurance. And on trips to the beach I only take a towel and sun lotion."

Marbella brings some happy memories for me. I was once dining with Paul Schofield, a Thomson Holiday representative and he'd ordered 'Chef's Surprise.' I played safe and opted for a mushroom omelette.

The waiter placed a plate in from of Paul, who asked, "What is it?"

"Chris de Burgh, Sir."

Paul was by now poking his lunch around his plate. "Sorry," he said to the waiter.

"What did you say it was?"

"I think it called, Lady In Red, Sir."

Collapse of me and Paul, much to the waiter's consternation.

By the way, the surprise was not a lady in red but Beef Stroganoff.

MAJORCA

News presenter ***Kirsty Wark*** says her worst holiday was in sunny Majorca and she's vowed never to set foot on the island again.

"I went to North Majorca in February, just two days after it had snowed for the first time in 90 years. It was so damn cold that we had to buy two fleeces, hot water bottles and hiking boots."

She pulled a face and exclaimed "Never, ever again!"

John Prescott MP was holidaying in the island with his wife Pauline, taking with him the camcorder he'd purchased in Singapore, a few months earlier. They hired a car and went high up into the mountains and found an extraordinary church in complete isolation. "It was perfect," said John. "Just the spot for me to try out the camera and I wondered if they would let us film inside."

The pair of them decided to see if anyone was about in case they needed permission. The place was deserted, so they returned to the car to collect the camera. It had gone.

"I couldn't believe it," said Mr Prescott, "We never heard a sound and had only been out of sight of the car for two or three minutes at most. We thought we were miles from civilisation. It was bizarre."

In the monastery at Valdemose you can see the island's most hallowed relic, the piano on which Chopin composed some of his nocturnes.

Groups file past in respectful silence, except once, but let the island rep. Tom Crichton, take up the story.

"Suddenly we heard a hideous jangling sound. One of the women in my group had climbed over the barrier and was banging out, Yes Sir, That's My Baby, on the venerable piano.

"The attendants, aided by two monks, pounced before she got to the chorus. When we were in the bus she said to me.'What was wrong? I was only trying to liven the place up."

I was returning from a business trip to Majorca and was sat beside the cartoonist ***Bill Tidy***. We chatted easily and he asked what my husband did. "He plays the saxophone," I told him.

"Do you want me to draw a cartoon for him?" he asked.

I was obviously delighted but had nothing for him to draw on. Suddenly I remembered the map of the island which had been presented to me by the Majorcan Tourist Board. I unfurled it from my flight bag. The back was virgin white. "Will this do?" "Perfect." said Mr Tidy and proceeded to draw a wonderful cartoon for Ray. Now that was a present that impressed him. Certainly made the obligatory tee-shirt or key ring look small fry.

Three months later I'd decided to take a quick three day trip to the island with my five year old son, to check out the hotels in Magaluf. As we made our way from Palma airport, there was a horrendous storm, with torrential rain and gale force winds wreaking havoc along the seafront.

Adam was looking out of the window, then turned to me smiling radiantly as only a small child can. "Look Mummy," he said, "the trees are waving at us."

When we checked in the hotel we were informed because of the storm, the water had been cut off. "Any idea how long for?" I asked. Sharp intake of breath "Oohh, could be 'till Thursday."

It was now Tuesday. A holidaymaker in his early twenties was stood nearby. "It won't affect me," he drawled, " I've brought an electric razor."

VALENCIA

The mountains of this region are breathtaking and they so enamoured the actor ***Billy Murray***, that he decided to buy a holiday home there.

"We have a beach nearby and all my kids were taught to swim there."

He continued: "I used to invite hordes of friends and relatives out there, often hiring a mini-bus so we could all travel together. It's amazing but as soon as I reach Calais I can feel all the tension lift from me."

"One year we'd all just settled in when the phone went. It was to tell me my dad had been taken seriously ill, and would I return home immediately.

"Tragically he died two weeks later but I was at his bedside."

SWITZERLAND

S*arah Kennedy* went to St. Moritz courtesy of the Daily Express.

"I did quite well on the nursery slopes," said Sarah, "probably because I had a blonde, bronzed instructor all to myself. On the last day he asked me if I was ready to try the mountain. I got to the top and managed half-way, I had to crawl the rest of the way down on my hands and knees. Probably the most embarrassing moment of my life. I know it sounds silly but I thought I was falling off the edge."

Which reminds me of a lady beginner who had 'frozen' half-way up a rather steep, nursery slope. The rest of the group were heading into altitude sickness territory, husband included, and they'd just left her. She was terrified, so I snow ploughed across, took off her skis and helped her 'walk' down. It was really just an excuse, for to be honest, I was nearly as scared as her. That instructor screaming 'bend ze knees, bend ze knees', will haunt me forever.

Notice in a Berne Hotel:

"If you have any desires during the night pray ring for the chambermaid."

A businessman in Kent, had to visit Geneva for an important conference. He had just collected his keys from the desk, when he noticed two rather large black ladies doing the same. The lift was quite small and the three of them just managed to squeeze in. They pressed the buttons but it didn't budge, suddenly the overload light went on and one of the ladies turned to him and said, "There aint no way you gonna travel with two fat mommas tonight baby."

Realisation dawned, it was the American singer ***Ella Fitzgerald.*** Now the conversation he'd overheard at the desk made sense. They were asking the concierge if 'Oscar' (Peterson) had come in yet and commented how well he'd played the previous evening.

Swiss Travel brochure: "If you feel like participating in a sightseeing trip to Geneva, you are welcome to it."

Dame Elizabeth Taylor has a 10-bedroomed mountain top Swiss chalet, in the jet-set ski resort of Gstaad. When her children were young she was a regular visitor, but the kids are grown up so, in 2000, she has decided it was time to put it on the market, as she hasn't visited it for over two years. She says: "It's taken this long to decide to sell as it holds so many memories."

So for you all who are looking for an away from it all retreat, it's on the market for £7.5 million. A snip, I'm sure you will agree.

THAILAND

D*on McLean*, said; "When I visited Thailand my wife fell madly in love while we there - with a baby elephant - It would come every morning to our hotel and she would feed it a banana. She would peel it then hand the skin back," he giggled, "That's the elephant not my wife!"

Actor ***Nejet Salih*** and his wife wanted a special honeymoon as they hadn't been able to go away when they got married, due to the punishing schedule working on the set of Eastenders. At the time he was playing a central character, the cafe owner and was recognised constantly, so they wanted an exotic location where he hoped he wouldn't be noticed.

"When we arrived in Bangkok, there seemed to be people everywhere. All hustle and bustle. Suddenly a tiny Thai lady came up to me, bowed and said, 'I see you on TV when I go to England.' I was amazed," said Nej.

The hotel they'd booked was in Pattaya, so for the three hour drive they hired a car.

"What an experience." he said, "For a start they drive on the left, but they drive like madmen, so you need a great deal of nerve."

A few days later they thought they'd go to see a Buddhist temple. It was perched on a mountainside and meant climbing innumerable steps to get there. Naj. said, "There were 290 steps.

I counted them, but it was worth it for the unbelievable views and we got to meet some Buddhist monks. The whole thing was absolutely great, a real touch of the East and no-one should miss the Grand Palace." He went on. "I know what I was surprised at, the number of Chinese who were visiting. They all travelled in groups and their leader seemed to be constantly blowing a whistle. In the lift they would all pack in together, overloading them something rotten, but they refused to get out even when the doors wouldn't shut!"

I agree with Nej. the King's Palace is quite breathtaking also some of the delicacies you are offered in the restaurants. Fancy fried Python? or maybe crocodile soup. Or would you be a coward like me?

USA

Language causes problems throughout the world and it doesn't have to be foreign. You can drop some real clangers in America.

Never call anyone 'homely' in the States, it means 'ugly'. And never, ever offer to help 'wash up', it means you'd like to assist them in their ablutions. Oh, I don't know though! You would also do well to avoid mentioning suspenders, American men wear them to keep their trousers up and vagrants have the misfortune to be called bums.

Other variations include lift versus elevator and pavement versus sidewalk.

Fraser Hines, the actor famed for his roles in Doctor Who and Emmerdale, was talking about the time he visited St. Louis on a promotional tour. "When I arrived the press were waiting for me and one of the questions was, 'Will you be visiting the Red Light district while you're here.' I was obviously more than a little surprised by the question, so answered by saying, 'What's the Red Light district?' Next day I was headlines in the local newspaper. It said: " Fraser Hines asks about the Red Light district."

When the band ***Slade*** were invited to America at the height of their fame, Polydor records had arranged transport to be waiting at the airport for the band and the crew.

All the crew managed to get through immigration and customs before any of the band members, so they made their way to the area they had been told transport would be waiting.

They were impressed. A black, stretch limo was parked just outside the entrance. The crew asked the driver if it was for the band Slade and he affirmed it was, so they all scrambled in and headed for the hotel.

A few minutes later having cleared all formalities, the band were discontentedly stood outside the terminal, surrounded by all their equipment stacked up on the sidewalk.

They couldn't understand where the crew had disappeared to and were becoming increasingly agitated at the non-appearance of their personal transport. A burly, perspiring, pallid man, wearing a Yankee tee-shirt and jeans approached them.

"You guys from Slade?" he enquired.

Noddy Holder nodded, asking if he was their driver.

"Yep," he said, "follow me."

They did as they were told, heaving and lugging all their luggage and equipment for over a hundred yards, where they were faced with a large black transit van.

"Right, you lot. In you get."

"What about the equipment?" asked Noddy.

"You'll have to load it yourselves." said Mr America.

"That stuff weighed a ton." said Noddy, "so we were not too pleased with having to load it all in the van. It didn't leave much room for us."

"We climbed in and sat among the gear and cases, all the time cursing the crew in no uncertain terms."

He added: "To put it mildly, we were not very enamoured with the record company's travel arrangements."

In the meantime the crew had arrived in style at the hotel. Two hours later the band were met with disbelieving stares when Noddy, followed by the rest, tumbled out of the back of a transit van.

A member of the stage crew explained: "We were all waiting in the foyer for the band to arrive, not realising they were having to manhandle all the equipment and ride shotgun in the back of a van."

Slade were told they had to be ready to meet the press twenty-five minutes after arriving.

"We were jaded, joyless and jet-lagged," said Noddy, "and definitely not in a mood to be pleasant and charming to the assembled hacks."

"But," one of the band confessed, "we were treated like royalty for the rest of the stay and we had a highly successful tour, so we soon forgot the unfortunate beginning."

"Did you ever get your stretch limo?"

"Oh, yes. For our return trip to the airport we had a stretch limo entirely at our disposal." He gave a wicked grin and added. "The crew went in a transit van."

ARIZONA

Another of those special places where I can sample my favourite type of holiday.

Being pampered on a guest ranch. I visited the Tanque Verde outfit and on the first morning we were told to saddle up and get ready to go for a breakfast cook-out. As we were riding though the Arizona landscape, I saw a Road Runner bird, the State's emblem. I was intrigued, I had no idea there really was such a bird, especially of such significance. "What sort of noise does it make?" I asked the craggy cowboy riding beside me. He gave a wicked grin and answered: "Beep, beep." - as I'm sure you all know is the sound made by the cartoon character, Road Runner as he's whirling along the road.

There were many more memorable exploits but I'm saving them.

Mary Nightingale is a girl after my own heart. She decided a ranch would be the perfect location for her honeymoon in April 2000. She said: "We first flew to New York to get married, then flew to a ranch we'd rented and spent most of the time riding. It was wonderful but I must admit it was very brave of Paul, my husband, who is really a producer and director and definitely not a horseman, but I needn't have worried, he thought it as wonderful as me."

BOSTON

You all know what the longest place name in Britain don't you? Thought you would. But can you say it and more importantly, can you spell it? Oh all right Clever Dick, there's always one! But, do you know what it means?

Are you ready for this? St. Mary's church by the pool of the white hazel trees, near the rapid whirlpool, by the red cave of the church of St. Tysillio.

Well that's what a Welsh friend told me anyway.

And it's:

Llanfairpwllgwyngyllgogerychwrndrogwlllantysiliogogogoch

There's a similar type of name in America, well similar insomuch as very few people can pronounce it. It was dreamed up by a Red Indian tribe, years ago for a lake just outside Boston, it's only forty-five letters, but I think even more tongue tying. It's called - Now concentrate because I will say this only once.
Lake Chargoggagoggmanchauggagoggchaubunagungamagg.

CALIFORNIA

While motoring though the state we were told a lovely story by another a holidaymaker from Edinburgh. We met at a filling station outside Carmel, which is between Los Angeles and San Francisco.

He told us :"We were filling up yesterday when a young man, who was cleaning my windshield, noticed my accent and asked where I came from. I told him I was a long way from home. Scotland. The boy looked a bit startled. Scotland? he asked me. Yes, that's right, I told him. Bonnie Scotland, so he asked me how long I'd been over here. I told him six days. The young man looked absolutely flabbergasted and exclaimed: Gee, how did you pick up the language so fast?"

By the way a visit to Carmel is a must. They don't allow traffic lights, neon signs or plastic flowers. It's quite a large town and even though the tourists go there in droves and most are on a, 'will I spot ***Clint Eastward*** or ***Doris Day***' trip, it still retains a calmness and tranquillity that is quite unique.

We went for lunch there, finding a small cafe off the main thoroughfare and ordered fish and chips. The owner came up for a chat. "I recognise that accent," he said. It turned out he was also from Yorkshire.

No wonder he was a dab hand at the frying game - Oh, well please yourselves.

COLORADO

"My first ever skiing trip was to Mammoth in Colorado, " says ***Jilly Johnson***. "I think it rates as my all time favourite holiday. Although I didn't learn to ski until I was in my 20's, I am very adventurous. On this holiday I discovered moguls fields - runs for advanced skiers where you have to swish around huge ice mounds. I wasn't nearly good enough for that sort of challenge, but it was such a thrill I couldn't resist it, but as you can guess I overdid it and fell flat on my face, which meant a trip to the hospital. It still didn't spoil my holiday. I came out and had another go."

FLORIDA

Do you know what the Americans call Miami? 'God's waiting room.' That's because of the large retired population that have settled in the city.

Which reminds me of Mrs Watson who came to see me in the shop to let me know her friend had bought an apartment in the state.

"Don't ask me why she decided on bloody Florida," said Mrs Watson. "It must be something to do with the quality of life over there. I mean," she leant conspiratorially over the counter. "They choose to clean their busses you know."

On my first visit to the state I saw a newspaper article reporting on a hotel fire. The Fire Chief's name was a beaut.

Bum Farto. It was! Honest!

I made a note of a local law while in the Sunshine state. Unmarried women are not allowed to parachute on a Sunday. So there!

I love Florida, but I remember returning home after my first trip and was swapping stories with my neighbour and his six-year-old daughter, who'd been over the previous month.

"I told you, you'd enjoy it," he said and nodded towards the young girl, still wearing her Mickey Mouse ears. "But I bet you weren't as impressed as our Alison."
he said.

"I bet I was," I answered confidently.

John smiled. "After the holiday and she'd gone back to school, the teacher asked her what things she'd seen. So she announced to the world the thing that had impressed her the most.

"I saw granddad take his teeth out."

Disney, eat your heart out.

Glen Murphy, star of TV's 'London's Burning,' visited Orlando with his wife and four children, but he had a rather inauspicious start. "I felt frustration and anger after our journey to Orlando. It took us 19 hours because of bad weather and delays. To cap it all we got lost on our way to the hotel in Florida. We were driving around for over two hours, then we found out the Howard Johnson Hotel was only 18 miles from the airport. When we eventually arrived there wasn't a kettle in the room as we'd been promised and we needed one to sterilise baby Emilio's bottle tops and warm his milk. I was really fed up." said Glen. "Then we found out the restaurant was closed for renovation."

The following day, feeling refreshed the Murphy's headed for Disney World's Magic Kingdom. "The thrill for me," said Glen, "was watching the sheer delight on my children's faces."

They then went on to enjoy all the other attractions of Florida. "One of my favourite theme parks was Boardwalk and Baseball. I showed myself up by trying to bat the ball as if I was playing cricket, but I soon got the hang of it. One of the best things about all the places, was the attitude of the staff. Nothing seems too much trouble and I must admit I soon forgot our horrendous journey to get there."

Lowri Turner says she thought her first beach holiday would be a nightmare, "Because I couldn't find anywhere to go shopping! I went to an island called North Captiva off the coast of Florida. The whole place only had two bars and one convenience shop. But I must admit by the time five days had gone by, shopping was not such a lure and I actually I felt relaxed and can now understand the appeal of beach holidays."

LAS VEGAS

The gambling centre, second to none. I found out that gambling started illegally in the Desert Inn Hotel in 1949. Stars flocked to this heartland of gambling and legends like ***David Niven***, ***Errol Flynn*** and ***Joan Crawford*** partied all night. When casinos were eventually legalised the public couldn't wait to get to those gambling tables at the Desert Inn.

It also became an entertainment institution. Sinatra's broadcasts from it were legendary, in fact everyone who was anyone in the industry appeared there, including Britain's ***Tom Jones*** and ***Englebert Humperdink***.

Arnold Palmer and ***Jack Nicklaus*** loved its golf course, as did Presidents ***Bill Clinton***, ***Gerald Ford*** and ***John F. Kennedy*** whenever they were in town. But in the year 2000, gamblers, presidents, and movie stars mourned the closure of one of the world's most infamous hotels.

But you can be certain that huge pink and green construction which dominated the strip for so long, will be replaced by an even bigger and more extravagant hotel complex.

The actor, ***Michael Pertwee*** says he loves the city, . "But I just can't resist the gambling, available twenty-four hours a day."

He admitted: "Twice I've left the place completely broke."

He then went on to recount the time he'd been to Los Angeles on business and as he had a free week-end, thought he'd pop across to Vegas and take in a couple of shows and maybe try to win a bob or two.

"I lost everything," he said, "In fact I was so broke as I was boarding the flight back to London I realised I didn't even have enough money to get my car from the Heathrow Airport car park."

Gloria Hunniford loves New York but also admits to thoroughly enjoying the sights and sounds of this gambling town. She hastened to tell us: "I never gamble though. I only go to visit friends and a chance to see some of the most spectacular shows in the world. Gambling," she said, "is a sure way of getting nothing for something."

This stirs a lovely memory I have of this spectacular oasis in the Nevada landscape.

I was draped across longer by the hotel's heart-shaped (what else?) pool when I heard a distinctive Texas drawl.

"Hiya Elmer. How ya doin' darlin'?"

"Nope I aint. It's no good honey, I think there's a hole in my bucket."

I must explain that as soon as you enter the portals of any gambling abode, you are handed a huge plastic bucket into which you can deposit all your winnings - like they say, hope springs eternal.

We used to watching fascinated as zombie like bodies, completely oblivious to the noise and bustle around them, twisted, spun, pulled and flicked to win that elusive fortune.

One evening we'd had dinner in the famous Dune's Hotel and Casino. Food is exceptionally cheap in Las Vegas and nearly all restaurants are situated on the far side of the gambling area. The presumption being you can't help but be tempted as you make your way to and from your meal.

I noticed two very large American ladies, sitting together at the slot machines. feeding them dollar after dollar after dollar.

One was clad in fluorescent pink from head to toe, including her lipstick and spangled tights, her friend was dressed entirely in canary yellow. Dyed, yellow hair, with the obligatory black stripe, was held together by a gigantic yellow plastic butterfly. A tent like creation, of barrage balloon proportions, wafted around her ample charms - oh and she was wearing lime green shoes and socks!

Suddenly the short, pink, grey-haired one, eased her bulk off the stool, saying: "Well that's it Hannah. I aint got no more."

"Nope," came the reply. "Neither have I. Let's go eat."

"But you've still got that dollar on the side there."

"Nope, I aint touching that. My son Harve gave me that for good luck. So it's staying with me."

With that she huffed and puffed her way off the stool. As these two giant blancmanges wobbled towards the exit, my eye suddenly caught sight of a vision in white heading my way. It was at least six-foot three, white, skin-tight trousers, exhibiting quite clearly, his manly attributes. A white shirt was casually opened to the waist and a white stetson perched jauntily on the back of white, shoulder-length hair.

He ambled along the passageway, the ornate silver buckle on his belt glinted in the spotlights - it was nearly as dazzling as the meteoric flash of his perfect teeth - He casually perched on the edge of the stool the overweight, yellow canary had just vacated. I saw the flash of a silver dollar as he popped it into the slot. He pulled the handle and wham, crash, wallop, dollars spilled everywhere. They leapt and jumped around the densely carpeted floor like sparkling fireflies. He'd hit the jackpot.

There must have been several thousand dollars spilling out over the tray.

Just think if the canary lady had spent her lucky dollar! Boy, is this a funny old world.

I got to know the late, irrepressible, ***Marti Caine***, quite well. She was a regular visitor to the Westfield Country Club, where my husband Ray was the resident vocalist and compere.

She was so excited when she got her first singing engagement in Las Vegas. We received a postcard, with a picture of the hotel she was starring in and a big cross marking her room. "Bet they don't think much to me hanging my knickers out to dry on the balcony," she wrote. She said she was having a brilliant time and one of the first punters she'd met was from Cottingham, the East Yorkshire village in which the club was situated.

When I met her about six months later, she told me about a couple she'd met by the pool.

"I got talking to a young girl called Sarah and she told me she'd gone to the local travel agents to book a two-centre trip to Las Angeles and Las Vegas for her honeymoon. Tickets and itinerary had been issued and there was just three days to go before the wedding. Now her fiancee had just stated up his own business and a very important job had come up which made it impossible for him to go away. It was a catastrophe, so she rushed to the travel agents to explain.

"They checked with the airline but there were no flights which could accommodate them on the dates of their choice.

"The girl said she was really upset and couldn't see a way round it, but suddenly had a brainwave. She made a phone-call and everything was sorted - Mum said she would go instead."

Marti said they were having a wonderful time and when she met them, they had already made over a hundred pounds on the one-armed bandits.

That has to be one of my favourite honeymoon stories, but I have another dozen which are even more bizarre - but next time.

My friend Sheila heard I was going to this gambling heartland and she told me she had a "sure-fire method of coming back with a small fortune."

I was all attention. "Tell me more."

"Easy," said Sheila, "You go with a large fortune."

Penny Smith and ***Penny Mallory*** were driving around the west coast of America for a TV programme and they took the opportunity to visit the Grand Canyon.

"It was absolutely amazing, a total high point for me," enthused Penny Mallory. I agree with her, but she wasn't snowed in for two days like we were. I was down to wearing my husband's black socks, with white strappy sandals, but my pictures are spectacular!

Anyway back to Penny who was waxing lyrical about the canyon, but she says: "I wasn't quite so enamoured with Las Vegas.

"It was really good to see it, although I never, ever want to go back there. Everything is just too huge - it's mad, and I thought stupidly big and flashy. It's a bit like Blackpool on steroids!"

Now that's a description I haven't heard before.

Both ***Aimee McDonald*** and ***Anita Harris*** started their showbusiness career in Los Vegas. Anita said "I was only sixteen and my parents were a bit worried but they let me go. I was only a chorus girl but it really set Aimee and me up for our future in the business."

A must on the itinerary of most visitors is a trip around the homes of the stars.

On the way you pass the 'Little White Chapel' which has an enormous billboard outside, announcing, 'Dynasty's Joan Collins was married here.'

One home you must see is ***Liberace***'s. It is an experience you'll never forget.

Did you know that the master bedroom has a reproduction of the Sistine Chapel on the ceiling?

There is also a museum nearby set up by Liberace, seven years before his death.

It is absolutely riveting. A treasure trove of glitz and smoltz.

There are pianos everywhere. One is supposed to belong to George Gershwin.

The costumes are breathtaking. Evidently for one, he was inspired by the Coronation Robes of our royalty, so for a Royal Command performance in London, he designed a replica. The chinchilla alone cost $60,000!

Also he owned what was reputed to be the largest rhinestone in the world. It is valued at $50,000.

Everyone was most respectful and it was lovely to see numerous photographs of his beloved 'mom' scattered around the house.

But visitors gaze in disbelief at the ornamentation of a show business legend.

Ostentation at its worst or best, whichever side of the fence you happen to be.

I found it quite amazing the reaction of nearly all the visitors. Yes, they were struck by the opulence and glamour, but the one comment you heard again and again was, " Weren't his feet big?"

LOS ANGELES

I remember reading a local newspaper report that two small boys had gone up to ***Paul Newman*** at a party and asked him; "Did you do Cool Hand Luke?" Mr Newman assured them he did. The youngsters looked at him a moment, then the chunky, ginger-haired one remarked: "Wow, that film really made you look young."

Alan Plater admitted that he once stayed - alone - at a hotel with mirrored walls and ceiling. "I was attending a conference hosted by the Writer's Guild of America. They explained to their visitors; sorry about the mirrors but the local hotel's bankrupt so we were able to get the rooms cheap. Room service was provided by a diner round the corner."

Kathryn Knight, columnist for the Daily Express had been to California on holiday and said she couldn't believe some of the things she saw. "I'd been shopping on the infamous Rodeo Drive and one shop was closed with a notice on the door which read: "We have been abducted by aliens. We will return."

Well you must admit it's original.

She also went on to say that: "Nestled among the boutiques and coffee shops was a store called Necromance. It looked like any other store," said Kathryn, "until you got close and saw the skeleton in the window, with newspaper cuttings about Chinese foot-binding."

"You have to knock to get in and once inside I didn't stay long. Thankfully, I managed to escape without buying a rat in formaldehyde, human finger bones, a dog scull or some extraordinary-looking contraptions that seemed best left unexplored.

"Still," commented Kathryn, "I'd love to see some of its other customers."

Another comment was about her scary brush with the vagaries of clothes shopping, US style. American sales assistants tend to work on commission and so pounce on shoppers like hungry lions, refusing to let go until they've mauled you into buying at least 12 things you never knew you needed. But let Kathryn tell the story.

"At the weekend, I went shopping with a friend who had merely intended to browse but, after a terrifying 15 minutes at the hands of Cheryl (five foot nothing with Nana Mouskouri hair), ended up at the till with a skirt, two tops and a shawl.

But even this was not enough to satisfy Cheryl's commission-hungry appetite.

'You're not buying the jacket?' she asked, snatching my credit card.

"I don't want it thank you."

"You should really buy it you know."

"I don't like it."

"It really suits you."

"I DON'T LIKE IT!"

Then a cautious pause before: "So what about the red top then? You're not buying that either?"

As Kathryn said: "It's enough to make Internet shopping look very attractive indeed."

Comedians ***Vic Reeves*** and ***Bob Mortimer*** hired a couple of motorcycles in LA so they could ride across the Mohabe desert in the 1990's.

"It absolutely poured down for four weeks," said Vic. "so we stayed in a house in a canyon, left our motorbikes in a garage and visited various boozers."

It was GMTV who suggested the two presenters ***Penny Smith*** and ***Penny Mallory*** off to the west coast of America on a road trip.

They hired an open-top vehicle and set off. Now Penny Mallory is a former National Ladies Rally Champion and now presents Channel 4's Driven, but even she admitted that she found driving in the states "a real challenge". But both girls found driving an open-top model an experience hard to beat and also "the thought that we could just take off whenever we wanted was quite exhilarating." But they added, "We did find it a bit scary at times. Take Los Angeles for instance they have these massive junctions with six lanes. There's traffic coming at you from every angle and it's a bit unnerving."

Ms Mallory was asked if they shared the driving. "Oh, definitely." she answered. "Penny Smith did all the driving really. She issued instructions and I just sat there and moved the steering wheel around. I actually don't know why she bothered taking her licence."

Penny Smith interrupted: "Because you like driving and I find it really dull because I can't look at things I want."

NEW ORLEANS

Where the whole business of jazz started.

I booked the playwright ***Alan Plater*** into a hotel in the centre of city. As a jazz enthusiast he insisted it was in the music quarter.

When he checked in he noticed a man already at the desk. He was obviously an important guest and he was insisting on the Presidential Suite.

Now the receptionist knew this suite was already taken, but she didn't say anything to the irate client. She asked him to wait as she wasn't sure it was ready, but she would make the necessary arrangements.

She rushed to the manager's office and explained the crisis.

Inspiration stuck. He arranged for a 'Presidential Suite' sign to be stuck on one of the best rooms in the hotel.

Later the guest was heard to say how he'd 'enjoyed every minute of his stay.'

But what Alan and I would like to know, but didn't like to ask, was, did they charge him presidential rates?!

Alan was disappointed in the music. "It's not a good place for jazz any more. The music is in aspic, a bit like a stately home, a tourist attraction for coach parties with cloth ears. On the other hand we went on a tour organised by the ***Louis Armstrong*** Foundation and saw houses where ***Buddy Bolden*** and ***Sydney Bechet*** lived. That alone was worth the price of the airfare. New Orleans is also the only place where our room had books of matches with our names on. I've still got mine. I can't bear to strike them."

Ah! Now we know who had the Presidential Suite!

NEW YORK

The stories about New York are endless, in fact I could probably fill a book about this diverse city on its own. They vary from the gregarious, hilarious and potty to the downright obscene. You either love it or hate it.

Take ***Pauline Collins*** for instance, she loves Ireland so I suppose it's understandable she doesn't think much to this city. "Ireland is the complete opposite to New York which I must admit I hate. You meet what you consider are normal ordinary folk and only to find out they're completely barking mad."

She went on to say: "It seems to me to be a city with their thermostats permanently turned on full and ready to blow."

Whereas ***Mary Nightingale***, a travel presenter on Wish You Were Here...? says she loves it. She started by saying: "I have a really fantastic job, but there are many times when I wish I was sitting at home and not on a sun-kissed tropical beach! The point is I can spend more than 120 days away from home in twelve months and inevitably the novelty of travelling wears off after a bit, plus I also get quite jet-lagged and there's the danger of becoming jaded by what I see, with the exception of New York. It's my all time favourite city." she enthused.

She then went on to say that in April 2000 she and her producer/director boyfriend were going to America so decided to combine a holiday with a marriage ceremony. "We'd been together for over thirteen years so decided it was about time we tied the knot and so booked New York's City Hall."

"It was a very low-key ceremony presided over by a Mexican woman and we couldn't understand a word. In the end when there was a silence we decided she must have finished speaking and took that as our cue to say our vows."

Richard Branson must have one of the best P.R's in the world. They never miss a trick.

His airline was due to start a new service to New York and large be-ribboned, personalised boxes were delivered to about a thousand travel agency managers in the country. Upon opening it we found it contained a large, succulent, red apple.

We get hundreds of pamphlets on new routes, new destinations and fares. All are looked at, filed away, sometimes remembered, but all agents, without exception, remembered the Big Apple.

Very clever.

I met him several times at promotions and he appears eternally cheerful and optimistic. I remember when his power boat sank while trying to beat the Atlantic record, he started singing, Cliff Richard's 'We Are Going On a Summer Holiday.' In seconds all the crew had joined in.

His zest for life is infectious. We could do with a few more extrovert characters of his ilk scattered around the world.

Nicholas Lyndhurst, recognised the world over for his part in Only Fools and Horses, is horrified of tall buildings. "I've got a pilot's licence," said Nicholas, "and I'm quite happy to loop the loop upside down in an aircraft but I'm terrified of sky-scrapers. I was visiting New York and went to the top of the Empire State Building and I was gripping onto the railings so hard that the tendons in my hands were hurting."

My friend Gary, a travel agent from Leeds, told me a lovely story about two, eccentric, middle-aged spinsters, who decided to book on the 'Splendours of The Fall', tour on America's East coast.

"When I went through the itinerary with them, they were a

bit dismayed to find they had to spend a night in New York before the coach left for the nine-day tour. I explained how interesting the city as and promised them they would come to no harm," said Gary.

"Upon arrival in New York they were met by a Jetsave rep. and asked if they'd like to book any sightseeing trips, as the tour coach did not leave until later the following afternoon. Maud, thought it an excellent idea as she could view all the famous landmarks from the safety of the coach, but her friend Clarice could not be persuaded. She said she would stay in the safety of the hotel.

Gary told me that Clarice had waved her friend goodbye, then decided to sit in the comfortable foyer for a while and watch the world go by. This small, bespectacled figure, was situated well away from the throng. Suddenly she noticed a commotion in the foyer and a lot of very large, black men were milling around the reception area. She felt uneasy so decided she would head for the comparative safety of her room. The lift was already waiting so she hurried to it and quickly stepped inside, only to find all the people she had been trying to avoid rushing to join her. Suddenly a voice boomed out. "Hit the floor lady." She slumped to her knees in terror. The man standing next to her realised what had happened and gently pulled the shaking lady to her feet. He explained: "In America, that only means you should press the required button for your floor." She said she felt extremely silly, especially as she looked around and found everyone was grinning at her. He gave her a kiss and said, "Lady, you've just made my day. Look I'm giving a concert tonight and I'll leave two tickets for you at reception." With that the doors opened and they were all gone.

"Clarice found out later it was Lionel Richie the famous singer, "But," she told Gary, "I'd never heard of him, so I never went to see if the tickets were there or not."

By the way, a bargain not to be missed is the cruise on the Staton Island ferry, which takes you along some of the world's most famous sights, with a full commentary and it's all absolutely free. An equally good bargain is the volunteer residents who will take visitors around the sights for up to four hours at a time, again no charge. Our fifty-something guide introduced us to the narrowest building in Manhattan - 9ft wide - and the White Horse pub where the author ***Dylan Thomas*** regularly drank himself into a stupor.

Claire Raynor and her husband Des. were at the top of the Empire State building, when a woman suddenly rushed up to her and said. "Oh Claire, how lovely to see you. I have this terrible problem...!"

I heard ***Derek Jameson*** tell a story on his radio programme about the 'Big Apple'. He decided New Yorkers were. "The rudest people on earth. It started at the airport. I never saw a smile. They treat everybody as if they were Al Capone. It was terrifying. You have fourteen year olds eyeing you up and down while brandishing guns."

"I checked into my hotel and after a quick nap and a shower I went to get a taxi, or as they insist on calling them cabs, and asked for 'The Corner Hotel, please, Greenwich Village.'

"Where?" grunted the driver.

"The Corner Hotel please."

"Never heard of it."

"I rummaged about in my wallet and showed him the card with the hotel's name and address on it."

"Aw, you mean the Corner Hotel." Then sped off and eventually we arrived safely at the hotel.

"I was more than a bit bemused by all this," said Derek "and couldn't resist commenting to a friend about his strange encounter. My friend burst into racous laughter. In fact it took several minutes before he quietened down. Then he explained. "He thought it was part of the name. People in New York are not in the habit of saying please for anything."

"It didn't improve when I was coming home," he said. "I was checking in at New York Airport and was watching while the passenger in front of me in the queue at the check-in desk was having a very heated argument with the clerk. I was really surprised as the clerk stayed really cool and sounded super efficient. When it was eventually sorted out the passenger walked huffily away. I went up to the desk and asked where the man was going. 'Don't you worry none about him,' he told me,' 'I bet you can't guess where his luggage is going."

When my husband and I visited the city with two friends, we stayed into the Milford Plaza Hotel, which was especially chosen for its location, just around the corner from Broadway and Times Square. That's about all it had going for it.

The room was in desperate need of re-decoration. There was no hot water, so we rang downstairs to complain.

"There's been a leak so we've turned it off."

"How long for, because we've been travelling for over twelve hours and desperately need a shower."

"Hopefully in the morning."

As it was only 4.30pm, that was some wait, so we had to make the best of a bad job. We had just two hours before we had to be setting off to see the world renowned singer ***Mel Torme*** at a supper club.

We arrived in an infamous yellow cab and however much we tried to engage the driver in conversation he resolutely refused to even acknowledge us - Except when he was waiting for a tip!

Upon arriving at our destination we were led to our table adjacent to a small stage.

How lucky, we all thought, to be so near the action.

The band made their appearance and proceeded to sort their music, while we tucked into our starters.

A ripple of applause started from the back of the room, building to a crescendo as Mr Torme made his way through the diners. He perched on a stool, three foot from our table. A beatific smile was flashed in my direction and he started to serenade the assembled throng.

I thought I had the perfect vantage point. Wrong! My head was now being 'buzzed' by the trombone player. The slide of the instrument was adroitly manoeuvred to miss my head - as long as I stayed perfectly still!

We paid the equivalent of £80.00 each for a meal and the sound of Mel Torme.

I think I was only marginally less entertaining than the divine Mr T.

Now I know why I was flashed that smile, not so much beatific as ...'I know something you don't know.'

The tatty hotel wasn't really that important as the location was perfect, which made up for a lot and it had a lovely Bell captain.

I got talking to him and he told me about an old lady who beat a mugger at his own game. She was sitting on a Manhattan bus, when suddenly an arm shot through an open window and seized her necklace. She clutched the man's wrist, the bus accelerated and with a yelp, the arm disappeared, leaving the plucky old soul holding his watch - a gold Rolex!

But I have a nice story about this much maligned city. I was wandering along Times Square when I came upon a tee-shirt shop I saw the perfect sweater and after rummaging about in my bag, found I was over a dollar short. The young man saw my dilemma and told me not to worry, I could have it at the price I could afford.

My hotel was only three blocks away and I had intended going back to repay him, but I never found the time. So you see, there are some lovely people in that most cosmopolitan of cities.

And having said that I can also tell an opposite tale. I had been delayed in Chicago's O'Hare Airport because of extreme weather conditions and so arrived in New York two hours after my connecting flight to Heathrow had taken off. British Airways pulled out all the stops and managed to get us on an American Airlines flight later that night, but we had about three hours to kill, so decided to visit a nearby bar.

We had ordered beers - no ice! and were sat chatting and enjoying our drinks, when after about twenty minutes the bartender came and hovered rather menacingly over our table.

"You orderin' agin?"

"No not at the moment thank you. We probably will later."

"If you aint drinkin', you aint stayin'."

We protested, explaining that we would definitely be ordering later.

His six-foot five frame, towered above us, like an eagle ready to pounce on his unsuspecting prey. He jerked a large, grubby thumb towards the door.

"Out!"

I started to giggle. It was so ridiculous. There was not another soul in the place. I decided I would try and reason with Gonzilla, but when I looked round, I had been left stranded by my so-called friends, who had escaped to the safety of the street and were now grinning inanely at me through the glass doors. So also being a devout coward I joined them.

Safety of the street - In New York!! Were we all mad?

Mind you, I think some of the people who dream up names for their businesses must sometimes be barking mad. But I have to admit they're nothing if not original. Take the guy who had named his setup, "The Rembrandt Ariel Company." I asked him why. His reply?

"Well, dat's sumpin dat'll tell the folks, dey don't just get a picture, dey get a great one!"

I couldn't argue with his logic.

Gloria Hunniford revels in New York. She confessed she adored visiting all these famous landmarks. “The Empire State Building, Sachs of Fifth Avenue, The Statue of Liberty, even Central Park is a joy,” she said.

An actor friend was visiting the ‘Big Apple’ and said he was woken every morning by his bedside phone ringing and this raucous voice announcing she was ,"Ada Clarke,” then putting the phone down.

He was very puzzled by this and mentioned it to an American friend, who burst out laughing and told him.

“You great Balony,” he said, “That’s the hotel receptionist giving you the alarm call.”

“Then why the hell doesn’t she say so, instead of just announcing, it’s Ada Clarke.”

His friend, still laughing, patted his arm reassuringly. “She’s saying ‘it’s eight o’clock, but don’t worry, you’ll soon get used to the Brooklyn accent.”

Which I’m sure will ring a bell with the songstress ***Lisa Stansfield***. She warns everyone to beware of their vocabulary if heading for the States. She explained. “I was in a hotel foyer and I innocently asked a bystander if he knew where the fag machine was.” She giggled and said “I don’t have to explain what fag means in America do I?”

This leads me nicely onto ***Bob Hoskins*** with a similar tale. He was chatting to Michael Parkinson and again commenting on the language on the other side of the pond being at times a snare for the unwary. “I fell into the trap as soon as I arrived in New York,” he told Michael, “I asked reception if they could get some fags for me.”

Selina Scott considers the French are probably the rudest people she’s met, but she did admit that the New Yorkers come a close second.

"No such thing as ladies first in that teeming metropolis, it's definitely survival of the fittest." she said.

"I was standing outside Central Station and trying to hail a cab. Again and again I stepped forward only to have some man push in front of me and leap inside. Eventually a cab driver did pull up right beside me, but just as I dashed for the door, would you believe two nuns materialised from nowhere and pushed in front of me." She admitted to feeling very deflated. "It looked like I would have to try the underground after all," she said. "Suddenly I realised the cab driver was waving the nuns away. The cab driver yelled at me, 'It's your cab lady'. I apologised to the Reverend sisters and climbed aboard. When I sat down I thanked the driver and admitted I still felt a bit guilty. I couldn't believe his answer. 'Lady,' he said, 'I'm a Jew, dem nuns don't cut no ice wid me."

Alan Plater says that many of his best adventures have been linked to films or television projects that never happened. "If I ever summon enough ego to write an autobiography, I'll call it Abandoned projects.' Probably one of the scariest times I ever had - theoretically scary anyway - was touring Irish bars in Jackson Heights in New York, researching for a film, about IRA arms dealers in the States. On the other hand, I was shown around by four armed FBI men, which gives you a definite sense of security.

"Music is a crucial element of my life, specially jazz. In a restaurant in Greenwich Village, the pianist, ***Ray Bryant***, played like an angel all night and I was the only one listening. New Yorkers can be zombies in these matters."

AIRPORTS

D*erek Jameson* says he must be the only person in the world who enjoys airport delays. "It gives me a few more hours free from the hostile natives. I adopt an Eastern philosophy. I always expect a five hour delay so I'm delighted when it's only three and-a-half!"

So I'm sure he would agree with the great Douglas Adams who once said, "No language in the world contains the phrase "as pretty as an airport."

Barry Appleby, the late cartoonist, famous for his wonderful daily, Gambol's strip in the Daily Express, told me his wife had seen some really cheap aircraft seats advertised and couldn't resist booking them. "They were two hundred pounds under the normal fare," he told me.

"It was quite the worst nightmare I could ever imagine," he confessed. Several changes and interminable waits in hot, uncomfortable transit lounges. The seats were crammed together. Drinking and eating were quite impossible with any degree of comfort or privacy."

Barry was so traumatised by the experience he drew it as a Gamble adventure and it was duly printed in the paper.

It succinctly displays his anguish, and the original now takes pride of place on my wall.

Libby Purves much prefers cruising. Flying does not impress her, commenting: "You stand around for hours in a busy terminal, walk along a steel tube and climb into another where you are strapped into a seat like a baby in a cramped highchair, and fed from a plastic tray."

"You sit in tedium for hours, with your legs bent uncomfortably and a faint smell of chemicals wafting past. At the other end, you queue interminably with your passport in another tedious building."

"All right," she concedes, "We can't do without air travel these days. But sometimes the heartless briskness of it all makes me long for time, and ships."

BRISTOL

Riot police had to race to the airport to calm holidaymakers who were held up for 27 hours.

Among them was funnyman ***Eddie Large***, who was travelling to Lanzarote to join up with his partner ***Syd Little***.

"It was a nightmare," said Eddie. "I rang Syd and he said he was sipping cocktails by the pool. When the police arrived people were shouting and banging their fists on the desk."

"Why, what went wrong?"

"Evidently it was originally delayed by a technical fault then when the spare part arrived, the engineers couldn't fit it."

"Did you have to stay at the airport?"

"We were taken to a country club for a meal and some were put up in an hotel overnight, but some passengers slept on the terminal floor and others just abandoned their holiday and went home."

GATWICK

Leslie Grantham, the actor said he was returning from a holiday in France and as they were getting off the plane, he noticed the man in front of him was clutching two plastic carrier bags stuffed with bottles. "I think he must have been sampling his wares on the flight for when we walked down the steps at Gatwick he slipped and dropped both bags. Ten litres of red make a nasty stain on the tarmac." He continued with a laugh, "I couldn't resist telling him. "Didn't you know that wine wont travel."

Overheard: "Yes, I'm having a two-centre holiday this year - Gatwick and Benidorm."

Bill Tidy, the cartoonist told me about two American tourists who had hired a car for their two week tour of Britain.

"They'd been gone a few hours when the phone rang at the hire desk in Gatwick. It was the AA and they told them,'We've one of your customers here and she's having a bit of trouble."Oh, dear,' said the girl, it's not broken down already has it?'

'I think blown up would be more accurate,' said the AA man.'You see they thought it had automatic transmission like her own car in America and she was doing about 70 mph on the M1 in second gear.'"

HEATHROW

Lionel Blair told me he'd been booked to appear on Dutch television and they duly forwarded him the flight tickets.

"I arrived at Heathrow and handed over the tickets and then the girl asked me for my passport. 'Oh Gawd, I've forgotten it', I told her and no matter how much I protested they said there was no way I could travel."

A supervisor was called and Lionel explained his dilemma, explaining he was appearing the following night on a live broadcast and needed to be there that day for a rehearsal.

The supervisor telephoned the Dutch TV company and told them the circumstances. 'Leave it to us for ten minutes,' they told her, in the meantime the British authorities had sanctioned his departure from London without a passport, so it was now up to the Dutch to accept him into their country.

The phone rang. It was the TV company. "No problem," they said, "We will be waiting for Mr Blair at Schipol Airport."

True to their word he was welcomed into Holland. After a very successful show, he met several influential executives who were very interested in his cabaret act. "I was very happy," said Lionel, as it looked like I could look forward to more gigs in the future, so, cheerfully boarded the flight home." He smiled mischievously. "Come on," I cajoled, "What happened?"

"I was stood at passport control to get back into Britain and the man behind the desk said, 'I'm sorry Sir, but there's no way we can let you back into Great Britain without a passport.' Adding, 'It's more than my jobs worth.'" - now where have we heard that before?! - "Anyway," continued Lionel, "He called over a colleague, who agreed with him. 'Under no circumstances can we allow you in.' I was now getting a bit desperate. It had all seemed so easy when I started off. 'What can I do? I asked them. They kept shaking their heads and tutting a lot. Then I noticed a wicked gleam in their eyes. It had all been a joke and of course they let me in, no problem. But I had to sign about ten autographs before they'd let me through."

A similar fate awaited ***Rex Harrison*** when he was coming over to appear in a stage play, but unlike Lionel he was playing the 'big star' and the immigration officials were not impressed.

"Do you know who I am?" he thundered.

Without looking up from the desk the official quietly spoke.

"No, sir, I'm afraid I don't, but don't worry if you've forgotten we can always look it up in your passport."

HONG KONG

Most of the airline pilots in the world agree that the old Hong Kong airport was one of the trickiest. All pilots have to practise on a simulator before they try the real thing. As it's an angled approach, so it has to be completely manual. A pilot told me, "It's challenging and stimulating, but great fun."

I was talking to ***Alan Whicker*** and he told me he was on a flight to Hong Kong when the pilot came over the intercom and said: "This can be a rather scary landing but there's nothing to worry about. If I were you I'd close your eyes, I always do."

I met Mr Whicker in Australia and he also told me that while he was queuing for the check-in desk at Heathrow, a lady came up and pulling his arm, asked: "You are Alan Whicker aren't you? 'I said yes I was. She then asked if I was on the Sydney flight, again I said yes. She looked up at me, gave a great sigh of relief and told me: 'Oh I'm so glad you're on the same flight as me. Your aircraft never crash do they?"

A stewardess told me about a Chinese businessman who had boarded the plane and after putting his attachè case in the overhead locker, settled down for the flight.

When he dis-embarked in Singapore he absentmindedly left his attaché case behind.

He was heading for the customs hall, when he was seen to turn ashen faced, spin round and start racing back to where he'd just come from. They would not let him on board to collect it, so a stewardess was despatched and soon returned with the missing case. As she handed it over he clutched it to his breast and started sobbing uncontrollably. He then explained. It contained over £200,000!

I never found out if he gave her a tip.

KLAGENFURT

While an acquaintance was browsing around the Austrian airport waiting for his onward flight, there was a surprise announcement over the tannoy, requesting all the passengers and personnel to evacuate immediately. "It was a bomb scare," he told me. "Not something you expect in the country of cows, mountains and leder-hosen. Anyway, we were ushered well out of the way and watched as bomb disposal teams rushed to the ladies toilets. We were told a cleaner had found a suspicious-looking device with a plastic case and wires attached to it. The emergency was soon over and the men re-appeared smiling broadly, the 'bomb' turned out to be an abandoned sex toy."

MADRID

Christopher Beeny, remembered for two television series in particular. 'Upstairs, Downstairs' and 'In Loving Memory.' with the indomitable Thora Hird. But Christopher is also an accomplished stage actor.

I saw him in one of my favourite musicals 'Stop The World I Want To Get Off.' I had seen the original production in London with Antony Newley. I had thoroughly enjoyed his portrayal of Littlechap and thought it couldn't be bettered, so went along with just a little trepidation, but an open mind to see this touring production.

I needn't have worried, Christopher Beeny put a whole new dimension to the part and acquitted himself superbly.

He is a lovely, modest man and we had a long conversation while taking supper with the rest of the cast.

Several years ago he was in a very serious accident and had to have several plates inserted in his leg, so whenever he passed through a metal detector in an airport he invariably set the alarms going.

"Normally," said Christopher, "they accept my explanation and I'm allowed on my way." He smiled, "Except once, in Madrid."

"Oh, yes, what happened?"

"I'd just checked my luggage through and was ambling through the electronic gate, knowing the alarms would be set off. I was trying to explain, even lifting my trouser leg to show the scars, but they wanted none of it and unceremoniously hustled me into a nearby room."

"I was bombarded with questions and then would you believe I was searched!"

"What, properly?"

"Properly! You'd better believe it! I was stripped naked and I think you could say it was a thorough search. They left not an orifice untouched!"

I shuddered. "Uugghh!"

"Quite," said Christopher. "They obviously couldn't find anything untoward and in desperation I kept waving my left leg about with all the relevant scars. But I still couldn't convince them. Probably because no-one spoke English - or so they pretended - and my Spanish is left to ordering a beer, two coffees or an omelette. By now I was more than a little upset, so decided I'd show my aggressive side and shouted I wanted an interpreter. Bad move," said Chris. "A pistol was thrust under my chin, jerking my head upwards and backwards, so swiftly I thought it was going to snap. I was terrified. The guards looked so menacing and the cold metal of the pistol was still pressing into my flesh. But, I was British and decided I was not going to stand for this sort of behaviour. Come on Beeny, I thought, you are an actor after all. I pushed the gun away and stamping my foot hard - I would have loved to stamp on the guards foot, but thought better of it - and demanded an interpreter was brought IMMEDIATELY! Eventually a stewardess from British Airways was summoned and after a long and very heated exchange with the guards, who un-nervingly kept looking my way while fingering their guns, then the one who looked most likely to eat me for breakfast, suddenly headed my way and waving his pistol motioned me to leave."

"God, what a relief, I grabbed my jacket from the back of a chair and I made my flight, with only seconds to spare."

"What an experience. I bet you couldn't believe you were actually sitting safely on that plane."

"You can believe it. I sat in a daze nearly all the flight home trying to recover my composure."

"Has it put you off flying to Madrid, or even Spain?" I asked.

"It did at first," he confessed, "But upon reflection, although they could have handled it a bit more delicately, with all the problems in the world today, it's maybe a good thing they don't take chances."

I told you he was a lovely fellah!

ST. LUCIA

I was stood waiting at the check-in for an inter-island flight and as normal I was asked my weight - a pair of scales was standing by in case you told porkies - As some heavyweights are prone to do, as often they are asked to catch a later flight.

A tall, heavily built man was in front of me and he was asked, "How much do you weigh sir?"

"With or without clothes?" asked a smiling passenger

"Depends on how you like to travel sir." was the deadpan reply.

AIRLINES

Definition of a bachelor.
'An airline pilot twenty miles from home'.
Don't blame me, Maurice, a Gulf Air rep. told me that one

After travelling on the Queen's Flight, the Duke of Edinburgh stepped onto the tarmac and was greeted by an official, who asked: How was your flight Sir?"

The Duke asked him: "Have you ever flown?"

"Oh yes Sir, many times."

"Well," said the Duke, "It was like that."

Leading British golfer ***Sam Torrence*** felt the sting of his wife ***Suzanne Danielle***'s tongue when he larked about with their three children during an unusually high-spirited flight between Edinburgh and London. Scottish born Torrence had stoically endured a two-hour delay before boarding the British Midland flight. While waiting to embark, Sam, Europe's Ryder Cup captain, took full advantage of a wide range of refreshing beverages thoughtfully provided to business class passengers to soothe the tedium. By the time the amiable Torrence had boarded the one-hour flight to Heathrow, he was feeling very relaxed and happy.

He was having a whale of a time larking about with his children, which involved among other things, leaning over the seats and making faces at them. This had them squealing with delight. He was very loud and this did not go down well with his wife as she strove to subdue the children.(Daniel 11, Phoebe, seven, and Anoushke, five.) She eventually snapped: "Sam stop being a child," and with a roll of her eyes heavenwards she sighed: "You're worse than the children."

The outburst had a remarkably calming effect on her moustachioed husband. He instantly ceased chortling and gurning and with an exhalation of defeat sat down quietly.

A stewardess said: "He was subdued for the rest of the flight. The rest of the passengers or the crew didn't mind his antics as it was all very good natured."

AIR CANADA

When I was travelling courtesy of an airline or tour operator, my seat was usually club or first class, but when my own holidays came round, I could only afford economy.

For over fifteen years I requested an up-grade. An airline rep. told me, if they have space, and the inclination to upgrade economy passengers, they'll choose someone who is neat and tidy and not carrying an Asda plastic shopping bag, or smelling of last weeks Brussels sprouts.

I think my husband I met all the criteria. I would humbly request an upgrade and they, not so humbly would say 'get lost' or similar.

Except on a flight to Toronto. We were subjected to critical appraisal, eventually, two minutes before boarding, we were told we would be upgraded to first class.

After belting up, I looked round. We stuck out like a sore thumb, most were in trainers and baggy, comfortable leisure wear.

A stewardess approached: "Bet you thought Christmas had come early," she smirked and continued serving us in that condescending manner throughout the flight. Now we were both grateful, but after a couple of hours I became so infuriated, I very, very nearly told her where to stick her smoked salmon.

When I returned home if a client came in for Canada, I would sell any airline except Air Canada unless it was the only suitable flight. So on my reckoning they lost about eighteen thousand pounds in revenue for that one snotty stewardess - There I've got it of my chest at last.

AIR GAMBIA

I wonder what the passengers of an Air Gambia flight thought was happening when they heard crashing noises and splintering wood coming from the front of the aircraft Evidently the lone pilot of a Boeing 737 had locked himself out of the cockpit when he went to the toilet. The door - it can only be opened from the cockpit side - had to be battered down with an axe so that he could regain control of the aircraft which he'd put on autopilot. Bet the cabin crew had to have some pretty nifty excuses ready. Can you imagine, a trembling stewardess would pick up the microphone and announce: "Ladies and gentlemen, I'm sorry but the pilot's locked himself in the lav. and he can't get back into the cockpit, but there's nothing to worry about, it's on autopilot,"

Panic, Mr Mainwairing!

AMERICAN AIRLINES

Just thought you might like to know that airline seats are finding their way into homes of the stylishly challenged, people are paying up to £300 for the seats, which always come in rows of at least two.

They're available because American Airlines are increasing leg room on their flights and have removed over 7,000 seats from its fleet. A sales manager in Texas (where else?) says he uses his for entertaining. 'We put them in the living room. When a game is on we pull down the food trays, put a beer on and watch in comfort. All my friends think they look really chic.'

Chic!? Well it was Texas.

Claire Raynor explained, "We'd never have holidays if it was left to my husband Des. He gets a sudden attack of childhood parsimony over flights. I want to fly first class, he'd rather go economy. To be fair, often the only difference is a curtain between you. So we've compromised. We do economy to Europe, club or first class on long haul."

The wonderful comic ***Spike Milligan*** was on television and he was asked about flying. He said: "I will only go if I can fly the Victorian way."

"What way's that?"

"You know, where the stewardesses would be dressed in bustles and crinolines and the crew would be attired in the uniform of the 12th Lancers. The interior should be wallpapered in maroon flock. The seats would be upholstered in buttoned velvet with floral damask curtains. A roaring coal fire is a must with the walls littered with oil paintings and you're surrounded by Jardinieres filled with potted palms and you are lulled to sleep by a trio of musicians. Preferably violin, cello and harp."

He grinned mischievously and asked. "What do you think to that?"

The interviewer, who had not stopped giggling throughout, gave a mumbled, "Brilliant. Yes, I think I like it, but I don't think it will catch on."

"Why?" queried Spike.

"It's a wonderful idea. But it's not really practical is it?"

"Trouble with you is, you have no soul." remonstrated Mr Milligan.

The late ***Marti Caine*** and her husband were on a flight to Tenerife. "Sat next to Malcolm was a woman with a screaming child on her knee." said Marti. "To pacify the infant she decided to breast feed it. It was not interested and continued to make the most horrendous racket. Suddenly I noticed a horrified look cross Malcom's face. What's wrong? I asked him.'Did you hear what that woman said?' I told him I hadn't." Marti then screamed with laughter as she recalled the reply. "Mal. told me she'd said, 'If you don't have your dinner now, I'll give it to this man 'ere."

Good job she wasn't sat next to ***Peter Tory***, columnist for a national newspaper. He concedes that there are few things more intolerable than settling down for a long flight only to find you are cruelly exposed to loud fractious children. "I would like to see an international smacking zone," he says, "about three miles up and of course the obligatory twelve miles from shore. Anyone could have a go, you needn't be related and I'm certain the screaming monsters would be terrorised into submission and hopefully we would have perfect peace."

I don't know about that, but what might work is an adult free zone at the rear of the plane, fully soundproofed. There the little darlings could be deposited and left there until touchdown. If you find that intolerable, let it be for adults like Mr Tory and me to relax and enjoy our flight in peace.

Birds Of A Feather,' star ***Leslie Joseph*** says, "I am always convinced that the plane is going to crash even though I know the odds are stacked against it. I spend the entire flight silently praying and the only way I can get through it is to take tranquillisers or get blind drunk."

The comedian ***Harry Hill*** was returning to London from Amsterdam after doing some promotional work. Suddenly a passenger became ill on the flight. "Is there a doctor on board?" asked a stewardess. No-one responded, so Harry obliged. "I'd trained for five years," he said, "But it was four since I changed careers, but I couldn't ignore the call could I?"

CONCORDE

A question in an exam for travel clerks asked:

Q: Concorde aircraft are the result of a liaison between which two major forces?

A: Britain and an aircraft company.

Oh well you can't win 'em all.

As I'm writing this the French Concorde had a terrible crash and they have grounded all the aircraft subject to an enquiry.

I hope it continues to fly as I've been lucky enough to travel twice by Concorde and I promise you it's awe inspiring. Do you know you travel faster than the speed of a bullet? Your meals, including caviar and smoked salmon, are served on beautiful bone china and your drink, usually champagne, is served in cut glass.

A steward told me that an Arab passenger checked in for his flight with three suitcases, weighing a whopping one hundred and fifteen pounds between them. Now the problems really started. He absolutely refused to be parted from them. "They," he informed the clerk, "are full of money. One million pounds to be exact."

Now that weight of luggage is well over any limit, so the girl suggested he bought an extra two tickets, so his luggage could travel as passengers and be strapped in with him. And that's exactly what he did. Not an eyebrow was raised when he was told that the fare for EACH suitcase would be over a thousand pounds!

I also spoke to CAA chief test pilot David 'Taffy' Davies. He told me;

"Anyone who can ride a bike and has passed a few 'O' levels can fly Concorde."

An Australian visitor to Britain wanted to see Concorde, so he and his wife took a tube out to Heathrow.

They were in luck, passengers were just checking-in for a flight to New York.

In one sudden impulse, he booked for trip to the States. His wife was not fired with the same enthusiasm and spontaneity - she also saw the cost - so while she pottered around the airport, he took a supersonic trip to New York.

She was waiting for him on his return and together they returned to their West End hotel on the return half of their cheap-day return tickets!

IBERIA

Iberia Airlines once ran a competition in which entrants were asked to complete the following phrase:
"Iberia Moneysavers offer guaranteed peace of mind because....
No-one can remember the winners slogan but the one everyone loved but couldn't use was;
"Because Joan Collins DOESN'T fly Iberia."

LIAT AIRLINES

This is the small inter-island flights which ply their passengers throughout the Caribbean islands.

We had been to Mustique and were heading for Antigua, but had to stop at St. Lucia to pick up four passengers.

One rather stout gentleman could not fasten his seat belt, so he asked the stewardess for an extension.

"We haven't got one. You'll have to dis-embark."

"I will not." said a rather angry passenger. "I have a very important business meeting in Antigua tomorrow morning and as this is the last flight, I have no intention of getting off. I fly this route regularly and I have always been given an extension."

"That may be sir" said the stewardess patiently, "but we haven't got one today and you cannot fly without a seat belt."

The gentleman was travelling with three other business associates and suddenly they all took off the belts holding up their trousers and offered to 'belt up' their colleague.

But all to no avail, the stewardess would not budge.

They pleaded, they cajoled, joined by several passengers and in the end they insisted they saw the captain. "It has nothing to do with the captain," she said. But they persevered and the captain was summoned.

Two St. Lucians near the front of the plane, stood up and shouted abuse at the Americans, saying: "If you had been black, the police had been called for by now and you would have been arrested."

The black man seated next to me started apologising profusely for his 'brothers' attitude. It was getting nasty. Then a large plump, black lady stood up and started laying into the two St. Lucians. She yelled: "He bought a ticket and they saw his size then, so they should have made arrangements. I think he should stay."

By now insults and abusive comments were being hurled from all sides. Passengers standing on their seats to emphasise their point.

The pilot appeared and motioned for the overweight gent and his friends to the back of the aircraft so they could discuss it rationally, but that didn't stop the tirade from all the other passengers.

We were in the throes of what was fast becoming a mini-race war, except it was black against black All over one white man, who was by now threatening to sue the airline for every penny they had.

No-one seemed to notice the pilot creep back to the cockpit and it was not until the propellers started whirring that the furore abated.

The American and his three friends had all disembarked but even though the problem was solved as far as our take-off was concerned, it did not stop the insults flying throughout the rest of the flight.

VIRGIN AIRLINES

The escapades of ***Richard Branson*** would probably fill a book on their own, as he's definitely not the shy and retiring type.

On Virgin's inaugural flight from Gatwick to Los Angeles, he arrived in day-glow wet suit, bare feet and as befits the head of a multi-million dollar empire, he toted a surf board under his left arm.

The press had a field day, which of course was the object of the whole exercise.

On the outward flight, an announcement came over the tannoy.

"Would Mr Richard Branson, please make himself known to the crew. There is a telephone call for him."

The whole cabin, erupted into unbridled laughter. The thought that R.B. had to make himself known was as ridiculous as the Queen shopping in Woolworths.

Hollywood took this genial entrepreneur to their hearts.

Stepping onto the hot tarmac. Surf board at the ready, he was met by local children, dressed up as plants and trees, arranged by the local PR to publicise the fact that Virgin were pledging a dollar, for every passenger flying that route. The money would go to a group in Los Angeles, who planted herbaceous borders. Honest!

They must have been absolutely delighted to see Mr Branson and his entourage disappear in puffs of carbon dioxide, as their stretch limousines ferried them to their luxurious hotel.

Sorry Richard, but you can't get it right all the time.

Virgin Atlantic are very proud of their First Class service and at one stage threatened their passengers with a trip to hell if they didn't agree that their service beat any other airline in the Business Class.

All you had to do was contact Mr Branson, give your reasons and claim the flight - nothing simpler - except nobody did. But I have a sneaky feeling there might have been a few try it on - even if it is the creme de la creme of travelling - if they'd found out that it actually was a very exotic location in the Cayman Islands.

Oh, by the way the offer was 'To Hell and back.'

In China you can take a stroll down Hell Street. They have a strange legend that ghosts do business there, so the shop keepers always have a basin filled with water nearby. If they suspect the vendor, they drop the money in the bowl. Genuine coins would always sink to the bottom, whilst pseudo money would float to the top.

HOTELS

Sarah Kennedy had been filming in the Midlands and was staying in a Holiday Inn in Birmingham. "I was tucked up in bed, when suddenly I awoke and thought, 'I am not alone,' It was quite eerie, so I swung my marbled limbs over the side of the bed and from underneath walked four pigeons. I nearly had a seizure as I have a thing about chickens and pigeons. The only thing I can think of, is that they climbed through my partly opened window during the night."

Thought you might like the notice board I saw in a Torquay hotel.

"Lunch will be served from 11am to the end of September."

Another favourite was placed on the window, so passers by could read it.

"Waitress wanted. Must be respectable until November."

The delightful and extraordinarily pretty lady *Anita Harris* told me a lovely story about the time she rang a hotel to book a reservation. "The reception answered my call and asked for my name, as soon as I said Anita Harris she flew into a tirade about having a famous person's name and what problems it caused. She went on to tell me her name was Shirley Jones. You wouldn't believe the things people ask me, she said. The most popular is 'You don't look old enough to be David Cassidy's mum.' She went on and on."

Anita said: "I was dreading checking into the hotel, but luckily she wasn't on duty, so we never came face to face."

Billy Connolly recalled the time he was staying at a hotel in Glasgow and his roadie was in a nearby room, when he - the roadie - decided he wanted another pillow. He rang downstairs to request one. About a quarter of-an-hour later there was a timid knock at his door. He opened it and couldn't understand why the dark haired beauty, in a very short skirt had not come bearing a pillow tucked underneath her arm.

Little did he know that a request for an extra pillow was a well known sign to reception for lonely visitors to require female company and what they had in mind was not something to rest your weary head on!

I was visiting London for a couple of nights to catch some shows and while walking towards the lift in the Central Hotel, I saw two girls in their late teens, jumping up and down and yoo-hooing very loudly. They saw my perplexed features and explained:

"There's no button on the lift wall, just a sign which says, 'lift operated from below.' so we thought we'd attract their attention."

I pointed to a small consul situated about three feet from the lift, with all the relevant buttons on the top.

"Aw, we saw that," said the plump, ginger-haired one, "but we didn't look at it properly 'cos we thought it was a rubbish bin."

But I can talk. That evening we'd booked for the comedy,'Run For Your Wife,' with ***Bernard Cribbins*** and ***Richard Briars***. My friend Gill was collecting the tickets from the box-office when I suddenly realised I was standing next to Bernard Cribbins. I was very surprised as I thought he would be in the dressing room getting ready for the evenings performance, which was only twenty-five minutes away.

I looked up and smiled winsomely at the beaming figure. Then the penny dropped. It was a cardboard cut-out!

After the show we went for dinner at a rather swish restaurant. I picked up the menu to see what was on offer. I saw 'Chef's special," but it had something written underneath in faint pencil. Thinking it might give me clue to the dish, I peered closer. I could just make out the words. It told me: "The head waiter's quite cute too!"

The following morning at breakfast, we were served by a charming, blonde, young man, who minced beautifully between tables.

We remarked how cold it was in London.

"Oohh, Duckies," he said, "It is isn't it?" Fair makes my nipples stand out it does."

Not a lot you can say to that.

The editor of one of our trade papers had been invited to a travel promotion party in London and had returned to his hotel just after midnight.

He was travelling to the Far East the following week, so had been to have his jabs. Typhoid, yellow fever, cholera and polio. To say he was feeling rough was an understatement.

He was desperate for sleep, so took a few aspirins and settled down.

An hour later he heard a tap on the door. He tried desperately to ignore it. The tapping persisted. He crammed the pillow around his ears. The tapping became louder and more insistent.

"Go away."

They did not. The knocking became louder.

"You've got the wrong room. Go away."

They were not dissuaded. The knocking became thumping. Wearily he climbed out of his cocoon and stumbled sleepily to the door. He opened it. There stood a waiter with a tray of canapès. He held them out to the guest. "Courtesy of the hotel sir."

John took them without a word. Closed the door. Placed them on the floor beside the bed and climbed back into oblivion.

He told me. "As far as I know they're still there."

Tom Jones, famous for decades for his provocative stage performances, at the age of 60, has said, he's putting those days behind him. "My skin tight trousers have been replaced by tailored suits," he said, "and when I'm on tour I always tidy my room. I don't want the hotel maids thinking, 'that Tom Jones is a slob.' So I make the bed, fluff up the pillows and fold the towels. I like the staff to think I'm a tidy chap, so the room has to look as nice as I can make it."

I was visiting the Costa Del Sol, inspecting hotels sold by Thomson Holidays. I was particularly interested in a new hotel in Fuengirola, which offered facilities for the disabled. I was being escorted proudly around the bedrooms and shown the wide doors, suitable for wheel-chair access and the handles in the bathroom. As we were going out the manager proudly pointed out the peep-holes inserted half-way down the outside door. "Excellent," I said, but then realised, it would not be a lot of use for the wheelchair bound, unless they could easily recognise belly buttons or grey, serge flys.

RAIL TRAVEL

Sarah Kennedy is a frequent rail traveller and usually tells her 'Dawn patrol' about the trials and tribulations she faces almost every time she travels by train. One week she said she'd checked the times twice with the rail company. The train arrived at Carlisle and stayed put. After half-an-hour, passengers were getting restless, and" said Sarah, "after an hour, threatening sounds were being made and after two hours, it was open revolt. Eventually a guard explained, "It's here for three hours. Weren't you told. The winter time-table starts today."

Carol Sarlor, columnist with the Sunday People was travelling from Scotland to London. She told her readers, "We were disturbed by a message coming over the tannoy: "We apologise for the overcrowding of this train. This is due to a large number of passengers travelling."

And one, which I'm sure you've all heard and for which the press had a field day; "We do apologise for the short stop, we are not sure when we can continue our journey as it seems to be the wrong snow on the line."

And as I'm writing this the BBC news just announced that Railtrack advised that there would be delays on a major line because: "There are the wrong sort of leaves on the track."

The late ***Roy Castle*** was always ready with smile and quip.

In fact only two weeks before his tragic death I received a letter, full of enthusiasm and fun. He told me how he was convinced he could beat that dreadful disease.

What a terrible loss. I can think of many occasions when we met, he was eternally cheery. One night he spent at least an hour showing my two left feet how to tap dance. He was full of stories and I fondly remember being in a small party after one of his hugely successful shows and he was telling us about the time he was working in London and used to catch the late night train home. "A typical city gent. got into the carriage, placed his umbrella, bowler and briefcase in the overhead rack, sat down and fell asleep within minutes of the train setting off. After about twenty minutes the train made an unscheduled stop in the middle of some countryside. It shuddered to a halt. Suddenly the city gent. leapt to his feet, got his belongings from the rack and went to the door, swung it open and stepped out into the night. Nobody said a word, then they saw an umbrella, then a bowler hat, followed by a briefcase being slung into the carriage, an arm appeared, then another as the man clambered back. He looked at everyone as he picked up his belongings from the floor. 'You must think I'm a terrible fool,' he said, and stepped out the other door."

Peter Tory, columnist for the Daily Express wrote many times about the vagaries of rail travel. He recalls the time he was travelling on a 125 on his daily trip into London, and as they were drawing into the station, a voice announced:

"Ladies and gentlemen this is your senior conductor speaking. We are sorry for the delay to our arrival in Paddington, but that is due to the fact we have arrived three minutes early."

He went on: "There is a train which stops at Romford in Essex which you can get on but which you cannot get off. "can't I get off here?" asked a rail traveller of my acquaintance.

"More than my life's worth, guv," came the reply.

"But there are people getting on."

"Passengers can get on, sir, but it is not really a stopping station, you see, so passengers are not supposed to get off."

Thus, the enduring puzzles of travel on British railways continue to puzzle us all.

There was a report the other day that a driver had "got lost". The tannoy sprung to uncertain life with the blattering announcement: "Sorry for the delay, ladies and gentlemen - and you're not going to believe this - but the driver doesn't know the way."

This event was almost as baffling as the occasion that passengers were told, as they remained stationary in Sussex meadows: "Sorry for this, ladies and gentlemen, but we're waiting for the pilot."

Peter says: "I have great concern for the apparent collective madness of the British railway system when an extraordinary proposal was leaked to the press.

"It was planned, we were told, to solve the problem of late running by unilaterally adding six minutes to the standard hour.

As far as we know, that secret scheme was implemented. It could explain a lot. And so, were we to expect that the grand new Shuttle, that elegant rocket which dives beneath the English Channel, was going to escape the lunacy? I fear not.

A lady who lives in Ashford Kent, was hoping that when the London-Paris Shuttle stops regularly at that station she might hop on it - as it pauses on its way from France, through the Chunnel, to Waterloo - in order to enjoy swift passage to work in the mornings.

Le Shuttle, she reasoned, would be faster than her usual commuting train.

"You'll need a passport," she was told at the local Shuttle office.

"What, to go to London?"

"Yes."

"That's fine," she said. "I'll use my passport."

There was a pause.

"Well, no, you can't anyway." she was told.

"But surely if I want to go to Paris I can on get the Shuttle at Ashford."

"Yes."

"But I can't get on it at Ashford - when it's going in the other direction - to go to London?"

"No."

"But I'm quite happy to use my passport."

"Your passport?"

"Yes."

There was a pause.

"No. No. You don't understand. If you want to use your passport to get to London, you'll have to go via Paris."

Do you remember the actor ***Tony Anholt***? He was the smoothie from many years back who starred in Howard's Way - and he really is as good looking off screen - He was playing the lead in Sleuth in Hull and I met him at the reception afterwards. He was telling me about the time he was rehearsing in Windsor and he had to rush back to London for some TV rehearsals. "Don't worry,', they told me, 'you can have some lunch while you're waiting for your train.' Marvellous I thought, so I managed to leave half-an-hour early, so I had time to eat my meal. I arrived at the station and made my way to the cafe only to be faced with a notice, scribbled on a grubby piece of paper which read.'Closed for lunch.'"

"What not even a chocolate bar?"

"Oh, don't worry. I decided to go to the snack bar only to be faced with another sign which read: 'Special reduction today. Cheese sandwiches."

I giggled.

"You may laugh," he said, "but all I could think of was my God, if they're reducing them how long had they been in that plastic bubble to gain that sort of recognition."

"So you starved."

"Not quite but I certainly didn't opt for cheese sandwiches, that's for sure."

He then went on to tell me about the time he was travelling to London.

"I was sat behind two middle-aged ladies and I couldn't help but overhear their conversation. It went something like:

First lady: "I had a what-do-ya-call it today."

Second lady: "Oohh!! You didn't!" Short silence, then.

"Well to tell the truth, so did I."

First Lady. "Well to be honest, I think I did."

Second lady: "I know, I expect you're the same as me. You have so many, you don't know if you're having one or not."

First lady: "I know. Tell me about it."

Second lady: (after sharp intake of breath) "oohh."

Tony continued. "They both slowly shook their heads and never said another word for the rest of the forty minute journey."

I'm sure there is someone, somewhere who has travelled in clean, warm trains which arrive punctually. Me? Don't ask!

Catching connecting trains is my nightmare. I step off one train only to hear a muffled 'The train now standing in platform eleven is the ten twenty four to London. It's now ten twenty. I race like an ostrich down stairs, along an underground tunnel, up stairs, across a bridge, sit in a carriage gasping for half-an-hour, only to be told. 'The driver hasn't turned up.

I once popped into the buffet at Doncaster station for a sandwich and a cup of tea. I noticed they had a special offer. "Special toady. 10p off ham sandwiches."

I don't know which I was most worried about, the toady or the old stale sandwiches.

About a week later I had two hours to wait on York station, so decided to check my bags into the luggage office and have a stroll around the town.

"That will be two pounds," said the man behind the desk .

I couldn't resist telling him. "I left some bags in Leeds last week and it was only £1.50 and I know for a fact it's only a pound in Sheffield."

I should have known better . He looked at me, raised one eye-brow and dryly remarked. "Well madam, if I was you I'd take them there."

Princess Michael of Kent has a story which appeared on her Internet column. She told everyone: "In 25 years I have only missed the Wimbledon Final and that because it was played on a Monday, due to rain that year. We had taken the Orient Express to Vienna, a magical journey along less used rail routes and to the most romantic of landscapes. Our son was ten at the time and failing to appreciate the view, played football with his slipper down the passageways, when not playing the piano in the 'saloon bar' carriage. He was discovered doing that at 5am."

I must admit the Orient Express is one train I couldn't fault. - although I didn't have small boys playing football outside my 'room' in the early hours of the morning!

It was a surprise trip arranged for some travel agents, arranged by The Association of British Travel Agents, to travel to the South of France for our annual conference.

The invited few were told to congregate at Victoria Station. When I arrived at the bustling station I had to bump my way through hordes of other commuters. I'm ashamed to say I felt distinctly a cut above the bustling melee; an impression enhanced by the tones of a Scottish piper guiding us towards the check-in lounge - so civilised.

Everyone was allocated a seat and a carriage. I was accorded the pleasure of Ibis, a glorious example of the coachbuilder's art dating back to the twenties.

As soon as I stepped on board the real world evaporated behind me. I took in my surroundings. I was embraced by perfectly restored marquetry, lush carpets and pressed tablecloths, you are instantly transported into another world.

I was offered Bucks Fizz immediately as I slipped into the soft embrace of a lusciously upholstered armchair. Honest! Everybody had their own free standing armchair, which you can push, pull, swivel and turn at a whim.

With the gentlest of jolts the train pulled out of Victoria, while I'm safely ensconced behind layers of glass, mahogany and Wilton.

Lemon jacketed young men kept topping up the Bucks Fizz. Eventually - after three top-ups - I put my hand over my glass and exclaimed, "No, I don't think I'd better or I wont be responsible for my actions." The pale, blonde, young man looked at me aghast and with a cursory shrug of his shoulders muttered. "As long as you don't take advantage of me madam." and shimmied away.

Well I was in my fifties and he must have been all of a gay-twenty-something. But I was soon carried away by the atmosphere and splendour and was in serious danger of enjoying myself.

If being a travel agent is considered hell, then I for one will be doing a lot more sinning in future - preferably on the Orient Express, Concorde, QE 2......

Oh, dear it's a hard life if you don't weaken.

I had booked ***Count Korab-Karpinski***, an orthopaedic surgeon in Hull, on a two- centre holiday to Argentina and Brazil.

When he returned he popped into the office to tell me about his exploits. He'd had a wonderful time and had particularly enjoyed Buenes Aries.

The Count often booked to go to London by rail but he confessed that after this holiday British Rail had gone up in his estimation.

I had to ask why.

"Well," he said, "When we were in Argentina, we were watching the television and they reported that an express train carrying 500 passengers had hurtled out of control through six stations. Evidently the passengers were amused to see a man running alongside trying desperately to jump on board. - until they realised he was the driver. Eventually a guard managed to halt it at the very last station on the line. What had happened was, the driver had got off to check the electric doors closing system but a guard, not noticing his absence, shut them and the train took off. They said passengers in the first carriage realised it was the driver running to catch his own train. On the television they also interviewed some of the commuters and a young girl, said she thought that everyone must know it was the driver and it would stop. But the train just went faster and faster, then nearly all the passengers started screaming - even the men."

Mr Karpinski said the girl admitted; "There had been absolute panic on board."

FINAL THOUGHTS

We have met a lot of people in a variety of places, so I suppose you could say the whole world is now a tourist destination but we don't all want to slope off to foreign climes when we have a spare week-end or two.

Take ***Jilly Cooper***, the novelist, says she's not at all enamoured with foreign climes.

"I haven't had a holiday for years," she says. "My excuse is that I don't have the money but actually I don't have the time either. I don't even take week-ends off. When I do go away it's to research a book. I don't take holidays because I can't bear to leave my dogs either. I suppose the closest I get to taking holidays is walking the dogs, picking wild flowers and getting drunk with friends."

Her daughter Emily agreed. "I think the last holiday was about eight years ago and that was in Normandy. I spent a weekend going around the house photographing whatever Mum was doing. She's crazy about Barbara and Mabel, her mongrel dogs, and she loves sitting in the dog's basket with them."

Someone else who admits to having no spare time for holidays, is novelist ***Jackie Collins***. "It's not unusual for me to take just two days holiday a year," she says. "My ideal break is being left alone with a load of books. When I lived in England I liked going to somewhere hot, but now I live in America I prefer to go somewhere cold. Providing I would be left alone to catch up on my reading, I'd quite like to take a family holiday in Hawaii."

I was talking to that very classy songstress ***Precious Wilson*** and she told me. "I've spent a great deal of my life in Europe, touring with my band. I live out of a suitcase, but I honestly love every minute. I even quite like waiting around. I've met some wonderful people on my travels, who make it all worthwhile.

"Nothing at all untoward?" I asked.

She thought long and hard and then admitted she couldn't think of one single mishap.

"Over the years everything has gone extraordinarily well. I can't even remember being delayed for more than two hours. In fact if I remember rightly, several times we actually took off before we were scheduled."

I was impressed. I told her I'd make sure she travels with my husband as he's your original Jonah. If anything's going to happen it will happen to Ray.

We chatted for a while longer then said our good-byes. Precious apologised for not being able to think of anything unsavoury I could put in my book and said she was disappointed not to be able to give me any juicy tit-bits, in fact she insisted on my telephone number so she could ring me if she thought of anything.

The call never came. Lucky old Precious.

TIPS

Travelling, in whatever guise can be a gruelling experience, but you can often waylay many problems with a bit of forward planning. So to finish off with let the stars offer you a few important tips to help make your holiday fire-proof - or nearly.

The BBC Newscaster ***Michael Buerk*** was a foreign correspondent for many years and travelled extensively.

"Any tips?" he was asked.

"Probably the best one is if you need to eat, drink or go to the loo, do it immediately, you'll not get another chance." He added, "You don't need to be a wonderful writer or very brave to travel the world, just have a very strong stomach. You get some weird and wonderful things to eat. I think the strangest thing I was offered was bat curry."

Caprice says: "Always take medicines such as aspirin and antiseptic also a big supply of vitamins.

"Other important things are rose water, moisturiser and concealer."

Judith Chalmers packs her suitcase very carefully. She said: "Be really tough about the amount of clothes you take. Put aside everything you'd like to take, then pack half. Limit the amount of shoes you take, probably maximum three pairs. You'll need an all-purpose pair and a pair of strappy sandals for the evening.

"Always take sunscreen, at least factor 15. Also pack all your creams and lotions in one plastic bag. I once had a silk blouse ruined when suncream leaked all over it."

Also Judith said she nearly came a cropper after a close encounter with a camel in Tunisia.

So she advises: "Always take along a first-aid kit on your travels. You can be caught out too often and in the past I was very glad of my antiseptic wipes, especially when that camel came up and bit me."

Race Davies: "If you wander off the beaten track, keep your trouser bottoms tied tightly to stop creepy-crawlies from running up your legs!"

Leslie Grantham advises: "Never carry your duty free in plastic bag, if you drop it, crash, you've lost the lot. Also don't be tempted to bring home a few bottles of wine which you loved on holiday. They very seldom taste the same without the sunshine. and the who-cares-what-time-it-is atmosphere.

"Experiment. Find one you really like when you're on holiday, then get a waiter to soak off the label so you can look for it in the local wine shops.

"Italy produces some of the best wines. Try Chianti Riserve and Piero de Monzi.

My last tip, don't go for the cheapest plonk just so you can boast to your friends, 'This was only 50p a bottle in a supermarket near our hotel."

Jenny Hanley: "Well I travel quite widely and two or three things which might help are; you know all those plastic pots in which you are served delicacies, when you've finished, pop them into your travel bag and they're perfect for keeping all your bits and bobs in, like earrings, buttons and spare change. And something else which might be of help. As soon as you arrive unpack and hang your clothes in the bathroom. When you have a bath and the creases should just fall away and if you have a really special outfit, pop some tissue paper between the folds when you pack it and again creases are non-existent."

Jilly Johnson: "Get insured! I wish I had listened. I now have a all-year long insurance that I take with my credit card, so if I have to go on a trip at short notice, I don't even have to think about it. I also have a small medical kit I take in my suitcase at all times."

Francine Lewis agrees. She says: "You should always take all your essential medical kit with you - especially if there isn't going to be a doctor around. I find air travel makes me feel quite bloated, so now I always take something to sort my stomach out wherever I go."

Billy Murray: "Just remember that most countries are not as wealthy as ours, so don't wear expensive watches and clothes when you go out. It's just inviting trouble. To those poor people, we look like millionaires ripe for the picking."

Mary Nightingale confesses that when she goes to hot climates like India, she eats lots and lots of chillies. "I've never had Delhi Belly and I'm sure it's got to do with the fact they're so hot, they kill any bugs."

"I also suggest you eat lots of yoghurt - the live bacteria are brilliant for sorting out unsettled tummies."

"But probably my main advice is to relax at all times, remember you're there to enjoy yourselves. Oh, and I always take my Gameboy Consul with me. I'm hopelessly addicted."

Emma Noble says "An absolute essential for me is my pillow - foreign pillows are often lumpy - also a sarong and trainers. I take far too many toiletries. But absolutely imperative are, Vaseline for your dry lips and an all-in-one face cleanser

"Also a mobile phone is now top of my list, after a disastrous trip where I contracted food poisoning and ended up in hospital being examined by a doctor with a fag in his mouth."

Jeremy Spake says: "Never mind the pillows and eye drops, top of my tips is take a spare pair of pants!" In fact," he said, "You should take at least five or six. A pair might split or if you get Delhi Belly like I did in the Maldives, you'll need every spare pair you have."

Anna Walker says: "The very first thing that goes into my suitcase are two swimming costumes. They form the basis of my holiday wardrobe. I team them up with shorts, sarongs and bright coloured flip-flops."

"It's also essential to take a pair of trainers or pumps for sight-seeing. If you're not comfortable on your feet, I guarantee that you'll soon be fed up.

"I also always take a good book and my portable CD player. Most aeroplane music is just too awful.

"Lastly, it's a good idea to take eye-drops on an the aeroplane. Planes are dehydrating so most take moisturiser and water, but then they forget about their eyes and they're equally important."

Simon Wright: "Always eat properly. So many young people go on their first holiday and go wild. They drink, and party and sunbathe and forget to eat. Instead, pace yourself, eat three meals a day, and that doesn't mean a greasy hamburger in the wee small hours after the disco has closed."

Me? Well I agree wholeheartedly with ***Jilly Johnson***. I've had so many heartbreaking insurance stories over the years. One had to re-mortgage his house, the second took to going around local pubs and asking customers to donate towards the hospital costs for her son who had been seriously injured on a motorbyke in Greece. Another who travelled up to four times a year to Majorca, but flatly refused to take out insurance. While enjoying the sunshine he suffered a burst appendix. He recovered but it cost the family dearly. After that, before any mention of the flights or hotels, he asked for insurance.

And ***Judith Chalmers*** is right, unless you're on a cruise or a really top class hotel, travel light. Over the years I have perfected packing and I never need a suitcase. I mix and match and roll the clothes, so they don't crease so much. They can all be accommodated in a hold-all, which I take in the cabin with me, so no interminable wait at carousels.

Anyway as they say, 'you takes your money you takes your choice. But wherever you go, I hope it makes you happy - Take care and remember, the rule for travelling abroad is to take your common sense with you and leave your prejudices behind.

NAMES IN ALPHABETICAL ORDER

ADAMSON Peter
AKROYD Christa
ANHOLT Tony
ANTHONY Lysette
APPLEBY Barry
ARNOLD Debbie
AYCKBOURN Alan
BEENY Christopher
BINCHY Maeve
BIRCH leila
BLAIR Lionel
BRANSON Richard
BRIARS Richard
BUERK Michael
BYRNE Peter
CAINE Marti
CAGE Nicolas
CAPRICE
CASTLE Roy
CHALMERS Judith
CLIFTON Bernie
COLEMAN Dez
COLLINS Joan
COMPTON Dennis
CONNELY Billy
COOPER Jilly
CORNWELL Judy
CRUZ Penelope
CURRY Mark
DANIELS Paul
DAVIS Race
DAWN Liz
DISTEL Sasha
DREYFUS Richard
FIELDING Yvette
FORSYTHE Bruce
GIBSON Mel
GRANTHAM Leslie
HANLEY Jenny
HARRIS Anita
HARRIS Rolf

HILL Harry
HINES Fraser
HIRD Thora Dame
HITCHINS Peter
HOLDER Noddy
HOSKINS Bob
HOWE Geoffrey Sir
HUNNICUT Gayle
HUNNIFORD Gloria
HURT John
JACKSON Betty
IREDALE Tony
JAGER Aude Herail
JAMESON Derek
JANSON David
JOHNSON Jilly
JONES Tom
JOSEPH Leslie
KEATING Caron
KEATING Ronan
KELLY Matthew
KENNEDY Sarah
KNIGHT Kathryn
KNOWLES Eric
LARGE Eddie
LEWIS Francine
LIPMAN Maureen
LIBERACE
LLOYD Kathy
LYNDHURST Nicholas
McCALL Davina
McDONALD Aimee
Mc LEAN Don
McMILLAN Terry
MALLORY Penny
MARSHALL Carolyn
MATTHEWS Francis -
MEDWIN Michael
MELLY George
MILLIGAN Spike
MOGGACH Deborah
MONKHOUSE Bob
MORTIMER Bob
MURPHY Glen
MURRAY Billy
NETTLES John
NIGHTINGALE Mary
NIGHTINGALE Mary
NOBLE Emma

O'GRADY Paul
OLIVER Jamie
PARSONS Lynne
PALIN Michael
PERTWEE Michael
PHILLIPS Leslie
PLATER Alan
PRESCOTT John
PURVES Libby
QUATRO Suzie
RAYNOR Claire
REEVES Vic
RICHARD Cliff Sir
RICHIE Lionel
RODDICK Anita
ROGERS Jean
SALITT Nejet
SARLOR Carol
SCHWARZENEGGER Arnold
SCOTT Selina
SHAW Tracy
SILVA Adele
SMITH Penny
SPAKE Jeremy
STANSFIELD Lisa
TENNANT Colin (Lord Glenconner)
TIDY Bill
TORME Mel
TORRENCE Sam
TORY Peter
TURNER Lowri
USTINOV Peter
WALKER Anna
WARK Kirsty
WELCH Denise
WHICKER Alan
WILLIAMS Simon
WILSON Precious
WRIGHT Simon

About the author

Dorothea lives in Yorkshire with her husband Ray. Her son, Adam is an actor.

Other books.

Buttocks, Boobs & Bedpans
A comic look at the medical profession in Hull and East Yorkshire (with cartoons)

The Shocking Truth
Another comic look at the folk of Hull and East Yorkshire, this time through the eyes of a Market Researcher. (with illustrations!)

All books can be obtained by writing to:

Buttercup Press,
Ferry Road,
South Cave
East Yorkshire HU15 2JG

Please add £1.00 for postage & Packing